Country Rugs

How to Design and Hook
Traditional Wool Rugs and Hangings

Pat Hornafius

with illustrations by Kay Carter

STACKPOLE
BOOKS

Published by
STACKPOLE BOOKS
Cameron and Kelker Streets
P.O. Box 1831
Harrisburg, PA 17105

Cover design by Kay Carter

Printed in the United States of America

First Edition

10 9 8 7 6 5 4 3 2 1

To my daughter,
Carrie H. Freeman,
whose enthusiasm, encouragement, time,
typing, and editing skills
made this book possible

Library of Congress Cataloging-in-Publication Data

Hornafius, Pat.
    Country rugs : how to design and hook traditional wool rugs
and hangings / Pat Hornafius : with illustrations by Kay Carter. — 1st
ed.
        p.   cm.
    Includes bibliographical references and index.
    ISBN 0-8117-3042-5 : $19.95
    1. Rugs, Hooked—United States.   2. Rugs, Hooked—United States—
Patterns.   I. Title.
TT850.H67   1991
746.7'4—dc20   91-17240
                                                                      CIP

Contents

Acknowledgments

Many thanks to Kay Carter, the illustrator, for her clear and concise illustrations, and to Miller Photography of Willow Street, Pennsylvania, for the fine photography.

And special thanks to Susan Bowser and Mary Karnes of the Elizabethtown Public Library for their extensive research for this book. No subject was too esoteric, no publication too far away.

Dear Reader,

This book will lead you step by step through the process of primitive rug hooking, introducing patterns of increasing complexity, from very easy to more difficult.

Chapter 2 fully describes the equipment you will need; how to dye, wash, and dry wool; tracing the pattern; and how to hook. This is essential reading material, but every pattern instruction is complete in itself.

Feel free to be creative. Nothing in rug hooking is written in stone. Adapt, change patterns, draw your own, let your wool supply dictate a design. You can accept or reject my methods and color preferences because your rug is yours to handle as you like.

Happy Hooking,
Pat

The Country Style

Country hooked rugs are called primitives. *Primitive* rug hooking? What immediately comes to mind is a badly made hooked rug, falling apart, with zany colors and a poorly drawn design. Not true at all. Primitive rug hooking is a method of working with wide strips of fabric (¼ to ½ inch wide) that are hand cut, machine cut, or torn. These strips are hooked to a base or backing of burlap, cotton warp cloth, or linen. The rug base is specially woven with bigger meshes to accommodate wider strips of cloth. Primitive burlap is 10-ounce evenly woven new burlap. Cotton rug backing, known as monk's cloth, is an alternative, as is linen foundation material.

The country women who first hooked these rugs were untrained artists, using as inspiration subjects found on the farm. This lack of artistic training produced vigorous, if somewhat unconventional, renderings of well-loved objects in a hooked rug design. The subject matter was rural, homey, and personal. Pets, homesteads, farm animals, and flowers were favorite subjects. Country rugs can be identified by their unsophisticated designs and wide strips of fabric.

Traditionally, hooked rug making was a salvage art. The ragbag was the source of fabric. "Waste not, want not" was practiced by all country people, and decorative arts originated from scrap usage.

Since odds and ends were used to hook rugs, antique rugs have many types of fabric in them. Long red underwear, checked farm pants, cotton dresses, and wool coats were all grist for the hooker's mill. Because these materials were of different weights, the rugmaker cut them in various widths to

1

equalize the strips. Accordingly, coat wool was cut thinner than dress cotton. When hooked all together, the varying widths kept the rug flat and even. To minimize fraying and approximate the bulk of heavier materials, cotton strips were cut almost one inch wide, then pinched together with the raw edges turned in (similar to seam binding) when being hooked. I watched an eighty-year-old woman who had hooked all her life use this technique. It is really very easy to pinch the wide cotton strip with the left hand under the burlap, folding the strip when drawing it through the foundation.

Originally, burlap feed bags were used as a foundation. Split open, washed, and stretched, the feed bag measured approximately 48 by 36 inches, dimensions that determined the size of the primitive hooked rug. Once it was bound, tacked, or sewed onto the frame, the finished rug size was a little over two by three feet. This size made a perfect hearth rug, bedside rug, or doormat. Back doormats, often the end scraps of the salvage chain, were made in multicolors and in crazy quilt designs. Very little thought was given to the design of back doormats, as they were subjected to daily use and dirt and so wore out and were discarded. Front doormats were special. Made in semicircles, often proclaiming "Welcome," they remained in good condition because the front door was used only for guests and funerals. Parlor rugs were turned over to avoid fading from sunlight and flipped to the front side when guests were on the way.

It was only after the Civil War, when jute was imported to America for use as feed bags, that rug hooking became popular. Earlier rugmakers in New England and the Maritime Provinces used linen tow bags as backing, but flax was difficult to process, and tow bags were scarce. With cheap and readily accessible burlap, rug hooking took off.

The foundation is one way to date a rug. Few rugs from before the Civil War remain. Not that the linen tow disintegrated with time, for it did not, but hooked rugs in most cases were considered only a functional item to be abused with normal wear. The exceptions were the bed rugs, or "rugges," that were hooked, shirred, or sewn for use on bedsteads. These rugs were extraspecial, not walked upon, and so remained in good condition throughout the years as a treasured item in the dowry trunk.

Since material for hooked rugs was saved for years, it is important to date a rug by examining all the fabrics employed. A rug cannot be older than the most modern fabric included in the rug. A rug using homespun and rayon, for instance, could have been made no earlier than the 1920s.

The use of commercial dyes can also place the rug in time. Commercial dyes were not available to farm folk until after the Civil War. Allowing time for clothes to wear out, the first use of these dyed fabrics would be in the last quarter of the nineteenth century. The use of all natural dyes would place the rug in an earlier period.

Colors and Fabrics in Antique Rugs

Country women used what they had on hand. Because hooked rugs were not particularly cherished, as were quilts, rugmakers used the end of the salvage chain—rags from the ragbag and foundations from used feedbags. This motley assortment led to an unplanned beauty. The wide assortment of fabrics from taffeta petticoats to worn homespun contributed to unusual texture and color in old rugs. I have examined Art Deco–style hooked rugs from the 1920s that combined checked blue-and-white homespun, pink taffeta, brown walnut-dyed farmer's trousers, and rayon stockings. Because large rugs required so much material, fabrics of all types and weights were thrown together in one rug, resulting in interesting patterns and textures.

Faded and varying textiles were used to fill the backgrounds with different shades of the same color, causing broken bands of color known as checking. This necessary use of various materials, with unexpected shifts of color, added an abstract appearance to the background. Country rugmakers gave no thought to changing color in hooking the large background area. It required the most fabric, and quantities of any one color were limited, necessitating arbitrary color switches.

Country people, with their arduous and frugal life, did not wear much wool. The washable cottons used for dresses, shirts, and trousers wore out first and were consigned to the ragbag. Sunday suits and shawls were sources for wool, but because of their cost and infrequent wear, they lasted a longer time and were not cut up until they were full of holes.

Farm women did not do much dyeing for their rugs. They

saved the more colorful fabrics for the rug center, consigning the drab shades of daily life to the backgrounds. Many times these neutral tones were mixed with bright (and scarce) colors in a hit-and-miss background, resulting in an interesting color flow. Again, rug design was not particularly color planned. What rugmakers had, they used in a color-intuitive manner, resulting in the unusual combinations we value today.

Early Hooked Rug Designs

Early rugs were hand drawn. Country women used motifs from daily life. The subject matter was derived from the farm: the old homestead with barn and animals, a well-loved pet, or flowers from the garden (particularly roses) appeared on hand-drawn rugs. Folk artists were untrained in academic art. Their rendition of a design was often crude and unrealistic. This personal vision created a drawing of charm and whimsy that reflected the importance of the chosen subject. Misproportion not only indicated a lack of draftsmanship but also emphasized the artist's priority. What was meaningful to the designer was drawn larger. Less important objects were diminished in size. A huge cow, tiny trees, enormous birds, and a small house could and did appear together on the same rug.

Sometimes the design became so far divorced from reality that the rug became abstract. Without stereotyped renditions of common phenomena to emulate, the artist's vision gave a surreal look to the hooked pieces. These are the favored rugs of antique dealers.

When imagination failed, rug hookers borrowed motifs from current publications. Magazines, a luxury, were not common on the farm, but Currier & Ives prints, the *Farmer's Almanac*, the Bible, and calendar art became sources of designs. Popular sports of country people, such as sulky racing, and national events inspired rug designs.

Printed feed bags complete with lettering offered predrawn designs and were hooked exactly as the pattern appeared on the burlap bag. The mill designs included cows, sheep, pigs, and chickens with the name of the feed mill and its location. Some rugmakers included the particulars of bag size and weight found at the bottom of the sack.

Amish quilt patterns were translated into rug designs.

Country rugmakers hooked actual feed bag designs directly on the burlap sack. When I asked one rugmaker why she did this, she answered, "I can't draw."

Small but amazing hooked rugs with great complexity of geometric design and brilliant color have been derived from such patterns as Bar and Broken Bar, Center Diamond, Sunshine and Shadow, Lone Star, and Roman Stripes.

Patterns for antique rugs were drawn on the burlap foundation with bluing (liquid indigo), which was used to whiten wash. You may have read that charcoal sticks were used to trace the design. At no time in my research have I discovered that such was the case. Not only are charcoal sticks dirty, but they are also soft, fragile, and flake off easily, an impractical method of transference. I have uncovered old boxes of patterns with an accompanying sharpened wooden stick stained with wash bluing. I have also found perforated brown paper patterns stained with bluing. The rug artist washed bluing over the perforated stencil with a rag, transferring the permanent dye to the burlap foundation. This technique created an arrangement of dots that lasted as long as it took to complete the rug.

The History of Commercial Patterns

Commercial patterns for rugs were first printed in Maine by Edward Sands Frost in 1868. An itinerant peddler, Frost was impressed by the hooked rugs he saw in his travels to New England homesteads. Having persuaded Grandma Benson of Biddleford, Maine, to sell her exceptional rugs, he took them home and translated the designs into zinc stencils made from wash boilers. Combining her flower motifs with border designs of scrolls and leaves based on rural versions of Aubusson carpets, he turned out a variety of rug patterns printed on burlap. The designs were greeted with such enthusiasm that Frost moved to Boston and set up a factory, hiring trained artists to design new patterns in the current fashion. Insecure at best in her drawing ability, the country housewife soon abandoned her artistic visions for those of the commercial rug designers, and in this way Yankee ingenuity killed native originality.

With the availability of inexpensive stamped patterns in country stores and mail order catalogs, rug hooking became a popular country craft following the Civil War. Spreading from the Northeast to the Middle Atlantic States, then following the homesteaders to the Midwest, rug hooking afforded thrifty and industrious housewives an inexpensive way to brighten their homes with the decorative use of scrap materials.

The farm community was dedicated to sharing. Just as quilt patterns were copied and shared, so were rug designs. Traced on light cardboard, these pasteboard patterns were passed back and forth at quilting and hooking bees. Designs, hand drawn by the artistic or traced from other sources, softened with use and achieved an almost abstract form with the blunting of detail. I have seen fifty-year-old patterns that were very smooth and worn at the edges, the shape rendered ever less distinguishable with repeated use.

Commercial patterns were traded, copied, and changed in this same community spirit. The Ralph Burnham hearth pattern, "Fireplace Scene in Olde Kitchen," itself a copy of an old New England hooked rug, was translated in rugs I have seen in Lancaster County into a variety of fireplace styles, mantel decorations, hearth rugs, and window treatments, each perhaps depicting the home of the maker. Adaptation of commercial patterns that were either purchased or copied was a common way of personalizing the rug hooker's product. These rugs cannot be considered folk art, as they are adaptations of commercial designs, but personal output was so distinctive that we can consider them transitional rugs.

Frankly, there are very few original folk-art rug designs. Farm women did not have art training: their art was self-taught. As a result, original rug designs were often crude to the trained eye. We cherish these hand-drawn folk-art rugs for this reason. Their naiveté is charming and unique.

The folk artist learns his craft at home using traditional methods passed down by generations. The primitive method of rug hooking has remained basically unchanged in technique and equipment for over 150 years. Although we no longer use the ragbag as a source of fabric, most of us started that way. With the intention of braiding a rug, I saved wool skirts, suits, and coats for years before I ventured into rug hooking. When I discovered that I hated rug braiding, there was nothing to do but learn to hook!

Getting Started

There are four essential items for making a hooked rug: the frame, the stand, the strip cutter, and a #2 primitive hook. You'll also need a pair of small, sharp scissors.

The Frame

Frames come in many designs. Antique frames were often a sawbuck construction made at home. Wooden rollers, kept in place and tightened by metal ratchets, held the foundation material and enabled the rugmaker to adjust the tension. The backing, stretched across the wooden beams, was laced to muslin sleeves attached to the rollers. This setup provided a working space of about 15 inches and required the finished rug to be rolled up on the opposite beam, starting at one end and working toward the other. Since only a small section of the rug was visible during the working time, an overall view of the rug was not possible. Sawbuck frames also required a horizontal hooking direction whereby straight rows went back and forth like a typewriter. You can spot this type of hooking in old rugs, thus identifying the type of frame used.

Another homemade frame similar to a quilting frame was made of ⁷⁄₈-inch wood pieces framed together by pins so that they could be taken apart and stored when not in use. The frame was supported by chairs, and the rug was clamped to the frame to achieve the necessary tension. Rugs made by this method were bound before the hooking began, as the tension

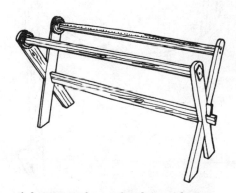

A homemade sawbuck-type frame was made to hold feed bag foundations about four feet wide, but I have seen one in Lancaster County that is seven feet long.

7

A Frazer Adjustable Frame tilts for any angle and adjusts for height. The foundation is rolled onto the rug bars and is held there with ratchets on each end.

was great enough to prevent bubbling of the burlap at the edges. I have never had success at binding the outer edge of my rug before beginning to hook. The burlap tension keeps changing and results in a lump at the finished outer edges. Then I have to rebind. I prefer to finish the binding last.

Today we can order wooden frames that are similar to quilting frames. I prefer a stationary frame, supported on a floor stand to maintain tension. A secure base allows speed and evenness of loops.

The Puritan lap frame can take small or large rugs with equal ease. A 15-inch opening with metal "prickle" bars (called carding strips) to hold the rug foundation tightly in place permits the rugmaker to lift and move the rug at will, repositioning each rug section in progress to the correct area. The Puritan frame also permits the rugmaker to begin in the center of the rug and work to the outside, keeping the tension on the burlap spreading outward to create a flat rug.

The Stand

If you are using a sawbuck or quilt-type frame, your stand is built in. If you use a Puritan lap frame, however, you will need to add a stand for smooth, speedy, and even hooking. Make your own, or use a small sturdy table. I found the very best stand at a flea market for seventy-five cents. It was a school desk with a wooden top. Just the right height (26 inches from the floor) with a shelf underneath for scissors and a hook, it is sturdy and solid. We drilled a hole in the top for the bolt and wing nut needed to hold the frame onto the front edge of the desktop. By loosening the wing nut just enough to enable the frame to be turned when reversing rows, my sturdy table ensures me fast, even hooking.

I like a stand that can allow a lap frame to turn. Keeping the frame in a rigid position means you have to twist and contort your arm when hooking in different directions. Sliding the frame to varying angles saves your arm and hand. Everyone has his or her own style of hooking, but my best rows are made when hooking away from myself in a straight line.

Whatever arrangement you devise, make certain that it is solid and stable. A frame bobbing around on your lap or rocking on a table is very limiting and results in lumpy hooking.

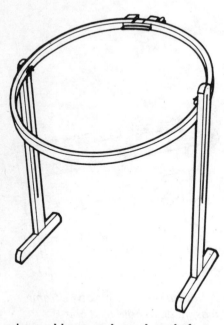

An oval hoop and stand made for rug hooking and quilting adjusts for height and angle.

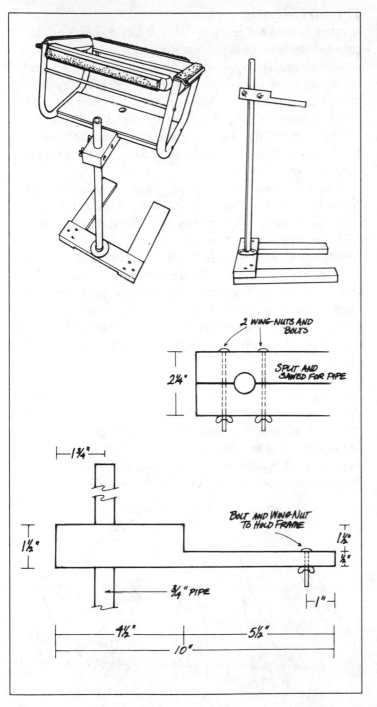

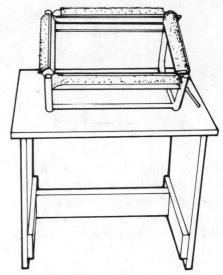

The Puritan lap frame on a stand ensures even work. Do not use the Puritan frame without a stand.

A 14-inch U-shaped wooden base supports my Puritan frame; I place my feet on it for increased stability. Insert a 30-inch pipe and metal holder (from the plumber) into the back splat and screw it firmly in place. The 10-by-2¼-inch cutaway extension that holds the frame slips over the pipe and can be adjusted up or down. Loosening the wing nut on the front portion of the extension enables me to turn the frame and change the angle of hooking.

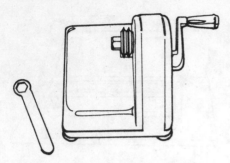

The Bliss Strip Slitter Model A is small, portable, and efficient. Blade sizes can be easily changed with an accompanying wrench. Use a #8 cutting blade for primitive rugs.

The Strip Cutter

A cutter is almost a necessity when making rugs. I originally cut fabric by hand until my calluses became too painful. Many primitive rugmakers prefer this hand-cut method or even rip fabric into strips. I do not like either method. It is very difficult in cutting ¼-inch strips to keep on the grain or straight of the material, which is vital to prevent the fabric from fraying or pulling apart when you are hooking. Wool fabric is too expensive to waste. Ripping weakens the fabric and leaves a fuzzy edge. Do invest in a cutter.

There are two cutters on the market that I have used, a Fraser 500-1 and a Bliss Strip Slitter. Both have their advantages. The Fraser 500-1 clamps onto a table and cuts faster. The Bliss has suction cups to attach to any surface and is more portable. Both have many sizes of cutting blades, but for primitive rugs I use mostly #8 (¼-inch cuts, two strips at a time) and sometimes #6 (slightly finer, $6/32$-inch cuts, three strips at a time). Some primitive hookers use ½-inch strips or ³/₈-inch strips, but I find these sizes too bulky to pull through the burlap foundation. Wide strips also lose more detail, although they certainly hook up faster.

The Hook

Hooks for primitive hooking have larger shanks and end catches. A #2 primitive hook has a crochet-type hook embedded in a wooden tool handle. Antique hooks were fashioned on the farm. A heavy nail was hammered flat and bent into the desired shape, then inserted in a wooden handle.

Find the handle that best suits your hand. A bulbous handle can be trimmed down until it is comfortable to grasp.

Foundation Materials for Your Rug

It is important to use a foundation of new material, as this is what will hold your rug together. Using old feed bags or cheap burlap for backing is a foolish economy. There are several types of foundation material, and you must decide which kind is best for you. Do not use an old feed bag for the sake of authenticity any more than you would pound out a hook from an old nail. Yes, there are purists out there (I was one myself), but considering the time and expense involved in making a hooked rug, plan to spend a little on the foundation. Old burlap from feed bags was throwaway material, poorly woven with thick and thin threads and improperly stored in rain and sun, which rots burlap. Purist that I am (or was), I hooked my first rug on an old burlap pattern found in a trunk. Brittle from age and heat, the burlap base disintegrated halfway through my making the rug, when the tension became tight and strained the foundation. Oh! Lost time and fabric! I mourned that disintegration.

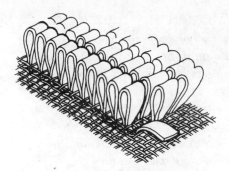

Meshes of 10-ounce burlap are widely spaced to accommodate ¼-inch strips. Skip two threads when hooking wide primitive strips (#8 cut).

New 10-ounce evenly woven burlap is my choice for small hooked rugs. I know that many current writers advocate using cotton or linen foundation material for the sake of longevity. Linen and cotton do not become brittle from heat or rot from moisture. For me, linen backing is woven too tightly for #8 cuts. It hurts my hand to draw up the loops through the closely woven material when the loops become packed as the tension tightens.

Cotton backing is so soft and floppy that unless you are making a large rug, I do not like the weight. The finished rug is not stiff enough to lie well on the floor.

As I mentioned, I like 10-ounce burlap, but don't get art burlap. Art burlap is woven with thick and thin spots to make an interesting surface. These spots weaken a rug base. Colored burlap is also something to avoid because the fibers are bleached before they are dyed. Bleaching takes the polish from the threads, making hooking more difficult.

I like the stiffness of burlap in the frame, I like the smoothness of the polished threads, which facilitates drawing up the loops evenly, and yes, I like the authenticity of the original rug base.

Measuring Your Wool

I use ounces in this book to describe amounts of wool. You may be using ripped clothing (and I hope you are) or small remnants that cannot be measured in yardage. Weights of wool range from 14 ounces to 10 ounces, and dye amounts are consistent with wool weight, not yardage.

If you are purchasing 12-ounce white wool, the yardage requirements are as follows:

36 inches, or 1 yard   = 12 ounces
27 inches, or ¾ yard   = 9 ounces
18 inches, or ½ yard   = 6 ounces
9 inches, or ¼ yard   = 3 ounces
6 inches, or ⅙ yard   = 2 ounces
3 inches, or ¹/₁₂ yard = 1 ounce

As most of my requirements fall within these measurements, you can readily make the conversion from ounces to yardage.

Use a small food or postage scale for weighing your wool. My scale has ½-ounce demarcations and weighs up to five pounds.

Wool Requirements for Your Rug

Because I use #8-cut or ¼-inch strips, I prefer 12-ounce wool flannel. This is dress weight—think of your pleated wool skirts. Coat weight is much thicker and more difficult to pull through the foundation meshes for my type of primitive rug. I have used just about every kind of wool and only draw the line at hard-twist wool worsteds and twills. They both fray a lot in the rug, and I hate that.

Be careful about using loosely woven tweeds. Most tweeds fall apart when cut into ¼-inch strips. Sad, but true. If you have tweed fabric and long to use it, try to shrink and mat it by washing it in hot water in the washing machine, agitating it, rinsing it with cold water, and drying it with high heat in the dryer. These are the foolproof ways to ruin most wools and render them felt, but in the case of tweeds, the process may tighten the weave enough to make them usable for a hooked rug. You will know when you cut them and pull them through the foundation. If they fall apart, so will your rug. Discard them!

Pendleton makes glorious 12-ounce wool flannel, as does Forstmann. Thirteen-ounce wool made by Dorr Mill is a bit heavy for #8 cut, but it is beautiful and comes in lovely colors. It is great for the smaller #6 cut, which is as fine as I hook. Woolrich makes a similar 13-ounce wool in solids and plaids. The plaids are 80 percent wool and 20 percent nylon; it takes dye well and handles like 12-ounce flannel. As it is very strong, it is good for backgrounds.

I never use polyester-wool blends; they do not take the dye and almost crumble when being hooked. Watch out for used clothing in flea markets or thrift shops. Examine the fabric content label before buying. Rip apart old garments and discard the heat-bonded interfaced sections—impossible to remove. Wash all usable wool with detergent in warm water, rinse, and dry for future use.

Running out of material is a tragedy that requires ripping. When figuring how much material I need, I calculate four times the area covered for ¼-inch strips (#8) hooked ¼-inch high. Some rug hookers need more, depending upon the height of the loops hooked. Five times the area should be plenty for everyone.

Make dye notations on your color chart in case you must dye more material. Remember that no matter how carefully you measure your dye, no two dye lots come out the same. Even with slightly different dye lots, the new material can be worked in by ripping out strips here and there in the finished field and replacing those openings with the new, similar color. Save the ripped-out strips to mix in with the new dye lot for the remaining unfinished area.

Dyeing

In every case, my dyeing instructions will use a TOD spoon to measure dry Cushing dye. The TOD spoon measures $1/32$ teaspoon and ¼ teaspoon. These are the only multiples I will refer to in the text, so do not be boggled by a given dye amount of $1/64$; just realize that I'm using this invaluable measuring aid and send for one.

The colors I refer to will be Cushing's Perfection Dyes. Permanent and relatively fadeproof (no home dye is sunproof), they are reliable and readily available. All my dye formulas are based on Cushing colors.

Please note that all commercial dyes are chemicals and must be used in well-ventilated areas. I always wear rubber gloves to work with dyes—you should, too. Most important, have a special set of pans to be used only for dyeing.

A few more items are necessary for your dyeing projects. A large heavy fork, kept especially for dyeing, will lift and move the wool in the dye pot. I use a large enamel casserole pan to spot wool for casserole dyeing and to tint with onion skins. Use this pan only for dyeing as well. I use a large amount of aluminum foil to cover the casserole pan for spot dyeing, baking wool in the oven, or simmering it on top of the stove. I also keep several Pyrex measuring cups to dissolve dye and to use when adding more dye to the dye bath.

Because I dye so frequently, most of my dyeing projects are done with a hot plate on a card table on the driveway. On rainy days, I use the stove to do my dyeing with the exhaust fan (ventilated outside) on full tilt. I have also installed a ventilating fan over my automatic washer so that when I spin out

Equipment Needed for Dyeing

rubber or plastic gloves
TOD spoon
W. Cushing & Co. Ordinary
    Type Dye
enamel, stainless steel, or glass pots
large heavy fork
enamel, glass, or stainless-steel
    baking dish for casserole dyeing
aluminum foil
Pyrex measuring cups
plain salt
white cooking vinegar
mild detergent
measuring spoons

Use only inert pots: glass, enamel, or stainless steel. These vessels do not interact with the chemical dye process, which would change the colors.

the exhausted dye bath and dyed wool, the fumes go directly outside.

You may not need all these precautions, but do be careful. I dye several times a week and take all the precautions I can. The natural dyes that I use do not require so many safeguards. Onion skins, marigolds, goldenrod, and walnut shells and husks are not poisonous. Some natural dyes are very poisonous, but I do not use them. A natural dye book will answer your safety questions.

Mordants

Mordants, from the French word *mordre*, or "to bite," are chemicals added to the presoaking of wool to facilitate dye take-up, change the color, and prevent fading. Derivations of metals, such as chrome, iron, copper, and tin, are poisonous and should not be used by the home dyer. Farm women used iron, copper, and brass kettles to gain the minute metal exchange needed for various colors.

Technically, vinegar and salt are not mordants. I will use this term here, however, as salt and vinegar aid take-up during the dying process. Use plain salt, not iodized, and common white cooking vinegar. Salt slows down the process and dulls the colors, whereas vinegar makes the take-up rapid and the dye brighter. It is an important distinction to remember when dyeing to mottle a piece of wool. Salt in the dye bath gives an even color; vinegar results in variegated color. Amounts should be adjusted to get the desired color and effect. I will be giving you more specific salt and vinegar measurements for each pattern I discuss later in the book.

Approximately one teaspoon of plain salt to one quart of dye bath (or one tablespoon to a gallon) is used for a very slow and even dye bath. If you have a water softener that uses sodium, add less salt. Salt dulls and "saddens" the color, which gives an antique look but inhibits mottling. Always add salt with the dye solution when beginning to dye.

Adding white cooking vinegar to the dyebath causes the wool to absorb dye more rapidly. This creates a very mottled effect and even leaves undyed spots on the wool. I like this effect for leaves and certain backgrounds. If too much vinegar is used, the wool looks coated with dye, much like natural indigo coats fabric. In this case, reduce the amount of vinegar—you want the dye to penetrate the fabric. Incomplete dyeing results in white edges along the wool strips when they are cut. You can add vinegar at the start of dyeing or, after the salt bath has done its work, at midpoint in the dyeing time (about fifteen minutes).

Using vinegar and salt together at the beginning of the dye process produces the best mottled effect. One tends to counteract the other. I use ¼ cup of white vinegar to one tablespoon of salt for about eight ounces of wool. This ratio creates a medium mottling that enhances a background but does not dominate it.

How Much Water for Dyeing

Throughout this book in each pattern's dyeing directions, I will be giving you the dye pot size and the amount of water required to facilitate a mottled dye look, as opposed to a smooth or even dye appearance. *The amount of water does not determine the color result.* The color is derived from the amount of dye and the amount of fabric.

More water in a large kettle allows the fabric to swim in the dye bath, exposing all surfaces to the dye for a more even take-up. Crowding wool in a smaller quantity of water creates mottled dyeing because the wool is not equally exposed to the dye bath. For maximum dye take-up, allow the wool to cool in the dye bath.

Preparing the Wool

Always presoak any wool that you are going to dye. Presoaking opens the fiber to the dye bath and permits complete absorption. I soak my wool in warm water for about one half hour prior to dyeing. If the wool has a hard finish or contains some synthetic threads, a drop or two of mild detergent will permit saturation. Do not use too much detergent or you will have to rinse it out before dyeing. Detergent resists the dye take-up.

When using old clothing, wash the ripped pieces gently in a mild detergent to rid the fabric of dry-cleaning fluid even if you are not planning to dye the wool. A hard, pressed finish and dry-cleaning fluid will prevent your loops from being

About Water

The quality of your water will affect the dyeing results. Hard water resists take-up. A little salt or vinegar is necessary to assist in take-up. Salt dulls the color and slows the process for a more even dye. Vinegar hastens the take-up and brightens the color. Test for hardness and adjust your salt-vinegar amounts to get the desired results.

Soft water (processed through a water softener) has already received sodium ions in the softening process, so be sure to cut back on or eliminate your additional salt, or your dye color will be very even and muted, if not dull.

The best choice is either rainwater or natural soft water. Each produces beautiful colors. Unfortunately, most of us do not have a rain barrel or live in a soft-water area.

In August, when the municipal water system is loaded with chlorine, it is difficult to achieve the perfect dye bath. I tried to substitute distilled water from my dehumidifier with poor results. It was necessary to add salt and vinegar to this pure water for any dye action to take place. Bottled drinking water was an expensive but satisfactory substitution on a temporary basis. Be sure not to pick up distilled water by mistake.

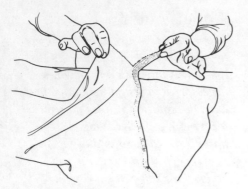

Tear off the selvage edges of your wool before dyeing. These strips can be used as dye testers before you immerse the large piece of wool in the dye bath.

Crowding the dye pot with scrunched wool will give a desirable mottled look to your dyed piece. This arrangement also presents pockets for spot dyeing with other colors.

bouncy. I wash all my old and new wool before using it so that my rugs are soft and clean. You can store washed wool without fear of moths.

Testing the Color and Immersing the Wool

Always simmer your dye before immersing the wool. It takes a little while for the dye particles to dissolve and mix evenly in the dye bath. When you are sure the mixture is ready, stir the dye bath, adding your salt and vinegar before immersing the test strip.

Now is the time to adjust your color. If it is too dark, pour off some of the dye bath into another dye vessel (for use later) and add more water to dilute the color. Leave the strip in the dye bath for a few moments before judging the outcome. A small piece will dye darker than a large piece of wool. To see what the dry color will look like, squeeze out the test strip in a handful of paper towels. The resultant color will be slightly darker when wet than when dry.

The wool needs to simmer one half hour to set the color and complete take-up. Removing the wool before it matures can cause it to fade later. If you are afraid the wool is going to be too dark with more simmering and take-up, remove the partially dyed wool to another pot, add plain water, and continue to simmer the prescribed length of time. You can always add more dissolved dye to the pot later to darken the wool if it needs it or spot it for more mottling.

Mottled Dyeing

Mottled dyeing is uneven dyeing, which in commercially dyed wool would be labeled defective. This light and dark variegation, so desirable in primitive rugs, when hooked will give the background a soft and mottled appearance not available in commercial yardage or by blending shades of wool.

Uneven dyeing is created by crowding the pan, stirring very little, and adding vinegar to the dye bath. Choose a dyeing vessel that is not too large, or your wool will have an even color. Crowding the wool in the pan assures that some of the surfaces will receive less dye than others. Stir once and lift the wool to be sure the fabric is fully exposed to the dye bath. Then let it simmer in a scrunched-up fashion until the dye matures. Directions on dye packets are for evenly dyed wool. We break these rules and gain a lovely mottled look that enables us to hook an entire background without changing colors, as the variegation is built in.

Spot Dyeing

If you think the dyed wool lacks enough variegation for an interesting mottled color, return it to the kettle after spinning it out in the automatic wash cycle. This damp wool retains the salt and vinegar mordant, so no more will be needed for the next step.

Again, crowd the wet wool in the kettle, adding an inch or two of warm water. Arrange the wool into small pockets, and pour additional dye into these areas. The wool crowded in the pan and at the bottom of the kettle will not receive the dye and will remain the same color. Only the pockets will become darker.

If you wish strong color for a very spotted effect (good for leaves and grass), use a strong dye solution. For a slightly mottled effect (good for backgrounds), dilute the dye solution with more water.

Spot dyeing is a good method to use when adding yellow, dark green, or blue spots to a basic green shade for leaves. These tiny variations of color increase visual interest in small areas, achieving color variety and eliminating the need for small strips of many colors. I hate tiny strips. They chop up the surface of a rug and weaken it.

Spot Dyeing with Onion Skins in a Casserole

Save the onion skins you have used in dyeing rust. I take out a cup or two after the shells have simmered for one hour, when the darkest color has been obtained. These used skins still have some dye in them but will not leave the harsh outlines on your casserole-dyed wool that fresh dry shells will. I like a diffused soft mottling, not a heavily spotted one, for rugs in the primitive style.

Arrange the presoaked wool in a baking dish lined with foil. I tear the wool from selvage to selvage to the width of the casserole to facilitate handling. Lay in one end of the long piece and sprinkle with a few shells. Sprinkle the piece with

Gathering Your Fabrics

Traditionally, rug hookers used scraps from the ragbag for their rugs. We no longer have a ragbag hanging by the back staircase—nor do we have a back staircase!

Today's fabric of choice for hooking primitive rugs is 12-ounce wool flannel. See "Sources of Supplies" for purchasing new 12-ounce wool flannel. Wool is soft, springy, resists soil, and dyes beautifully. It is expensive and sometimes hard to find in some parts of the country, but mail-order sources are very reliable.

I like to use plaids, checks, and stripes (even tweeds) that are hard to find except in used clothing. Haunt your local thrift shops, especially during sales day. Ask when they clear out wool garments in the spring. I buy men's plaid and tweed jackets and flannel trousers for twenty-five cents each at that time. You can spend the summer sorting, ripping, and washing to be ready for fall hooking. This is a country custom worth emulating.

Yard sales, consignment shops, and flea markets all yield used clothing. Mill end stores are a bonanza. Locate a friendly tailor who will save cut-off hems and cuffs for your tiny scrap needs. Being a scavenger is part of the fun!

1 teaspoon of salt. Fold the wool flatly in an overlapping fashion, adding more shells and salt to each fold as you smooth it in the pan. Continue layering the wool in the casserole, sprinkled with shells and salt, until the wool is completely used, ending with a layer of onion skins (think of it as onion-skin lasagna). Press down on the wool to be sure the shells are in contact with all of it. The presoaked wool should contain sufficient water to simmer or bake the casserole, but if it seems dry, add more water or just a little leftover onion skin dye. You want the original wool color to remain, only speckled with onion dye.

Cover the casserole with foil and simmer it very slowly on top of the stove or bake in the oven (Pyrex casserole dishes must be used in the oven) at 250 degrees for several hours. Add water if the pan becomes dry. Permit the casserole to cool completely before removing the wool. Then pick off those nasty shells, rinse, wash, rinse, and dry.

Use tan, oatmeal, or camel wool for the best results. Onion skin dye on white wool is too contrasting. Spot dyeing works well if you wish to further mottle wool dyed with a light onion skin bath (for, say, a calico cat). Wool mottled with onion skins looks great for borders, tree trunks, fences, and animal coats. The technique gives life to flat dull colors, casting a golden rust glow.

Overdyeing Colored Wools

Simmer the dye required (about $1/32$ teaspoon) in 1 cup of water plus ½ teaspoon of salt and 1 tablespoon of vinegar. If you are using several colors, prepare each color in a separate pan. Do not use vinegar with yellows and reds.

Remember the color wheel and avoid using opposites, for they will turn to mud when combined. Colors adjacent to each other on the color wheel work best. Blue and yellow on green wool . . . yellow and red combinations . . . blue, green, and violet blends.

I use this overdyeing technique for textured areas in my rugs: trees, leaves, borders, and any area needing a definite color mix. Avoid the technique for backgrounds. It is too chopped-up looking.

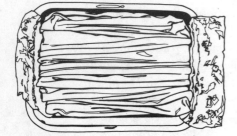

Presoaked wool, pleated accordion style, in a foil-lined casserole pan can be overdyed to simulate a plaid by alternating several colors of dye.

Pour alternate strips of different-colored dyes over the folded pleats. The wet wool will diffuse the dye, but the accordion pleats will prevent the dye from penetrating inside the folds. In this way, you will get a variety of values and colors.

Half-and-Half Dyeing

Another method of spot dyeing a large piece of material for a background is to spot dye half-and-half. You can use this method to mottle the background for "Little Guernsey," an upcoming pattern.

You will need khaki wool (8 ounces) for the "Little Guernsey" example, but spot dyeing any color will be effective if you want a slight graduation in color. Presoak your khaki wool. Add $2/32$ teaspoon of Dark Green in the bottom of a 2-gallon dye pot with 1 inch of boiling water plus 1 tablespoon of salt. Scrunch the wet khaki wool down in the Dark Green dye bath. Only the area touching the dye bath will absorb the color.

Now dissolve and simmer $1/32$ teaspoon of Khaki Drab dye plus 1 teaspoon of salt in 1 cup of boiling water in a small pan. Pour this hot dye solution on top of the khaki wool crowded in the 2-gallon dye pot. It will produce a half-and-half dark green and khaki-drab mottling on the khaki wool. Cover and simmer for one half hour. Keep checking the water level (which will be very low) to prevent the dye pot from becoming dry. Add a scant cup of water to the dye pot if necessary. If you add too much water to the bottom, the dark green will soak into the entire piece of wool and make your khaki wool too dark.

You want to dye only the bottom of the wool touching the dark green dye bath. The center of the crowded wool will remain the original color. The top half will be spotted with the Khaki Drab dye solution poured over the crowded wool. When you spin out the remaining water, you will see a lovely stained-glass effect of dark green, khaki, and khaki drab, which will hook into a varied and interesting background. The secret here is to prohibit an even take-up of dye on the top and bottom by not using too much water and arranging very crowded scrunched wool in the dye pot.

Washing and Rinsing the Wool

After simmering the wool for one half hour, permit it to cool in the dye bath before rinsing. Rapid changes of water temperature shrink and mat wool. Wool for ¼-inch strips must be soft and pliable to pull through the foundation. Matting wool is permissible, however, if you have loosely woven tweeds or

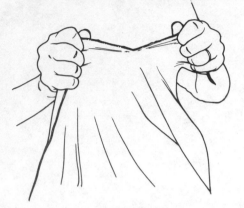

Rip the wool from selvage to selvage into 3- to 4-inch strips to obtain the straight grain of the fabric.

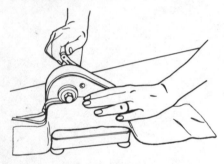

Gently guide the 4-inch strip of wool against the side and turn the handle. With a #8 cutter blade, you will produce two strips at a time.

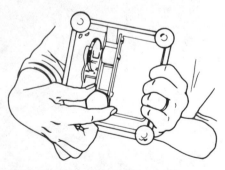

The pressure screw adjusts the tension of the cutting blade. Tighten until your strips cut apart. Too much tension can etch the roller.

basket weaves. They will fall apart during hooking without preshrinking.

Drain off the exhausted dye bath and dump the dyed wool into your automatic washer to spin out the water. Use the warm-water wash-and-rinse cycle to wash the dye residue from the wool. I add a squirt of mild detergent to the wash cycle to neutralize the vinegar and remove the salt. Do not agitate the wool, but permit it to soak for a few minutes in the detergent bath before spinning and rinsing. Be generous with water levels. The wool should float in the tub.

You can hand-wash and rinse small amounts of wool. Again, permit the wool to soak, and squeeze it to extract the water. Do not wring and twist.

I shake the washed wet wool gently after removing it from the final spin. You may line dry wool on a nice breezy day or hang it on a rack or shower rod to dry.

If your wool is lightweight or you wish to shrink it further, dry it in the automatic dryer. Remove the wool before it is completely dry and hang it on a rack to finish drying.

Cutting the Wool

If you are using ripped-up old clothing, washed or dyed, tear pieces into appropriate widths depending on the size of the remnant. For new wool, remove the selvage ends of your yardage, if you haven't already done so for dye testers, and rip into 3- to 4-inch strips. I use the entire 60-inch length when I hook to avoid all those cut ends appearing on the surface of the rug. If this length is cumbersome to you as a novice hooker, cut the pieces in half (30 inches) or thirds (20 inches).

Assemble, cut, and bag your wool strips before starting to hook your rug. I like to cut half the wool for my rug before beginning to hook. Keeping one half in reserve makes color matches possible if more dyeing is required. Wool cut into little strips is difficult to duplicate in color. Cut half of each color and place the strips in a clear plastic bag. Label the bag with a permanent marker so confusion does not reign. I always make a numbered color chart noting the area to be hooked, dye formula used, and amount of wool required, including a swatch of that particular color for future reference.

Tracing the Pattern

Whether using burlap, linen, or cotton rug backing, I keep a 6-inch extra margin around my designs when transferring the pattern so I can fasten it on the rug frame. If you are using a quilt-type stretcher frame, more margin may be necessary to attach the backing to the outside bars. Do not cut away the extra backing until you are sure that the pattern will fit the frame. If you are using a Puritan rug frame, 6 inches on each side will be plenty of margin.

Now that you have the proper size for your rug, with the extra margin around all four sides, you will trace the pattern. A grid design is provided with each pattern given in this book. To trace the design onto your foundation, it is necessary to increase the grid blocks to the desired size, keeping in mind that each block must be increased proportionately. In other words, a 1-inch block can be increased to a 3-inch block, which will triple the size of the finished design. To double the size of the grid and the rug pattern, increase each 1-inch block to 2 inches. If you are sure of your drawing skills, draw the enlarged grids directly onto the foundation material.

I use permanent markers when working with patterns. Permanent markers do not run when wet and will prevent your drawing from bleeding up through your rug in the event that the rug gets wet at some future time.

Be sure to draw the grid on the straight grain of the foundation so your pattern will not be crooked. It is difficult to hook straight lines on a slant. Pulling a warp (lengthwise) and weft (crosswise) thread when using burlap or running a colored thread through linen, following the weave, ensures straightness. Cotton warp cloth often has this colored line woven in.

Examine each block in the grid superimposed on your chosen design. Every block has a line running through it. Draw that line in the same direction and proportion to the grid in each block of your foundation. These lines will meet at the edge of every block, forming a new, enlarged design.

If you wish to see the completed enlarged design before marking the foundation, draw the enlarged grid on a piece of brown craft paper or draftsman's parchment.

Another reason to draw your enlarged design on paper

before transferring it to the backing is to avoid confusing grid lines and design lines when hooking.

When greatly enlarging a design, look at the completed design in its blown-up state to check the proportions of the enlarged pattern. Doubling and tripling is fine for most border and flower patterns, but animals can get out of hand.

An interior designer once asked me to make "Little Holstein" into a five-by-seven-foot rug for a breakfast corner. When I explained to him that the increased dimensions would produce a six-foot cow under the table, we decided on a farm scene!

If you increase your design on paper, you will then have to transfer it to the rug foundation. I use black typing carbon paper for transference. Place your burlap on a hard smooth surface—a cement floor or laminated-plastic tabletop. Wood surfaces may take the impression, so be wise in choosing what surface you trace on. Secure the burlap with masking tape. You will not be able to see the traced design on the burlap until it is finished, so be sure the burlap doesn't slip, dislodging the design.

Lay down your pieces of carbon paper on top of the burlap, totally covering the area you wish to trace on. Then lay the pattern design, corrected and perfect, on top of the carbon paper. Measure the outside margins carefully to be sure the pattern is on the straight grain of the foundation, 6 inches or more from each edge. Remember to get straight lines on the straight grain of the foundation, following the heavier lines woven into monk's cloth for this purpose or pulling a thread on the outside edge of the burlap horizontally and vertically. If you do get the pattern slightly askew, all is not lost, but it is much easier to hook up a straight row than to hook slantwise. Tape the paper pattern down to the foundation so it does not move.

Now we begin to trace. Using an old ballpoint pen or wooden meat pick (the size used for candied apples), draw over the paper pattern, pressing very hard to transfer the design. Begin in the center and work to the outside edges. Don't peek until it is completed, or you may dislodge the pattern. This job is a hand crusher, but do press as hard as you can. If the paper tears and you wish to save it, cover the entire pattern with 2-inch clear cellophane tape. This keeps your pattern usable for the future. Having transferred the design, draw around the outside edges with a yardstick or measuring square so your corners are squared off before you remove the pattern.

To be sure your pattern is perfectly rectangular, measure the paper pattern from corner to corner diagonally. These two measurements should be the same or your rug will be crooked.

Remove the pattern and carbon paper, and pray that the transfer is visible. You may peek at a corner before removing the pattern if you are not sure. Better safe than sorry.

After removing the carbon, I go over the carbon lines with a permanent marker to correct any mistakes and keep the design from brushing off while I'm hooking the rug.

Mechanical Enlargers

In this age of mechanical enlargers—copy machines, opaque projectors, and overhead and slide projectors—enlarging a pattern is simple.

A copy machine can increase your pattern to a certain limit, losing clarity as it enlarges the image. Enlarge your rug design to the limit per page size, then section off this copied image into pieces and enlarge each piece the same percentage until you have reached the combined size of the desired rug design. The completed enlargement will be fuzzy but traceable.

If you have access to an opaque projector, the design can be enlarged without worrying about sections. Cut a piece of craft paper to the size desired for the finished rug. Attach the paper to the wall with masking tape and move the projector away from the wall until the size of the projected design exactly fits the craft paper dimensions; then trace. If you are planning to use an additional border, draw this design on the craft paper first so you can adjust the center design to fit the remaining space.

Overhead projectors found in most classrooms require a transparent drawing. Trace your design on a piece of acetate and project it onto pattern paper cut to fit the finished rug size.

Slide projectors can enlarge as well if you have a transparency of the rug design. Again, cut your pattern paper to the

Materials Needed for Tracing a Pattern

yardstick
measuring square (24 by 18 inches, 45-degree-angle rule)
small ruler
ballpoint pen, pencil, or meat pick
fine black permanent marking pen
masking tape
brown craft paper or draftsman's parchment
black typing carbon paper
2-inch clear cellophane tape
foundation material

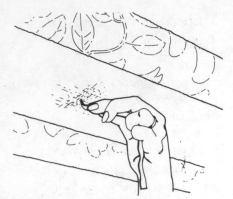

Hold the wool strip under the area to be worked with thumb and forefinger. You will feed the hook with this hand.

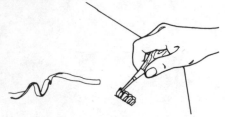

Hold the hook on top of the work with your other hand, grasping it as a baby holds a spoon.

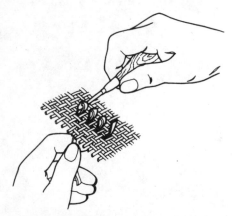

Skip two threads of the burlap and reinsert the hook for the second loop, drawing it ¼ inch high.

desired size, adjust the distance of the slide projector from the wall to fit the space, and trace.

This equipment for tracing is available in virtually every school library in the country. There should be no problem in going into the school and using it, especially if you have children in that school.

How to Hook

You have gathered your equipment, dyed your wool, cut your strips, and traced your pattern. Now let's learn to hook.

Place the pattern on the frame. If you are lacing the pattern to the edges of an old-fashioned frame, keep the tension tight. As you hook, the tension on the foundation will increase, but you don't want to start hooking on a floppy surface. You will need the same sort of tight tension when tacking a pattern on a picture frame. Using a Puritan frame or quilt-type frame allows the rugmaker to move the pattern at will and tighten the tension at that time.

Start hooking in the middle of your pattern and work to the outside edges.

Old-fashioned roll-up frames work from one end to the other. Begin at the far side and hook the design toward you. It will be necessary to unroll the foundation as you work and roll the finished portion onto the far beam.

When using a Puritan frame, adjust the stand so that the frame faces you at about table height. Place your feet firmly on the base of the stand to keep the frame from bobbing around and to give you something to pull against. Keep both hands steady for speed and evenness of loop height. If you are working without a firm stand, you are on your own. Good luck!

Insert the hook into the mesh opening, hook the strip below, and pull it up through the mesh opening to the surface. You are working on top of the rug. Draw the first strip end to a ¼-inch height or a little higher. Continue drawing your loops to the surface until you have completed a color area or have run out of strip material. Snip off the first and last pulls evenly at ¼ inch. That's all there is to it.

All ends begin on the surface and end on the surface. Snip

off ends ¼ inch high as you work. Try not to cross over previously hooked areas underneath. Doing so creates a lump and a loose loop under the work that could pull out later. Always draw your strip to the surface and cut if off when moving to another area. I snip off the top of the last loop to ensure a complete cut. By inserting your scissors tip into the loop to cut it, you could miss a thread and inadvertently pull out the finished strip when removing the unused portion.

Outline the area or figure you are working on before filling in its center to maintain the shape. Think of your pattern as a coloring book. Outline inside the drawn line and then color in. Single lines and tiny areas are hooked directly on the lines.

Some burlap will be visible underneath the rug. Hooking every third row of mesh will pretty well cover the burlap, and small areas of burlap in corners cannot be filled in without crowding the surface of the rug. The rug will be tight without becoming lumpy or hard packed if each loop is hooked skipping two meshes and each row is separated by two lines of burlap thread.

If you find that the strip is twisting as you pull the strand to the top, keep pulling much higher—4 to 6 inches than you want the loop to be. Then, with your other hand under the burlap, pull down the strip to the correct ¼-inch loop height to untwist the loop. This maneuver will not be necessary when you gain proficiency, but it does ensure nice fat loops for a beginner.

Is your wool fraying when you release it from the hook? Be sure to unload the strip from the hook by turning the hook downward so the crook does not catch the side of the strand. Think of it as pouring water from a cup; lift the loop, unload, and release the strip. This method eliminates the ripping action that tears out a warp thread and makes your work look ragged.

Always keep your hand under the foundation to adjust the height of the surface loop. If you find your loops getting uneven—and you may have some trouble at first—pull back slightly on the strip with the underside hand to make the loops a uniform height. Making uniform ¼-inch loops just takes practice. Here is where a taut foundation and firm frame stand to pull against will help you achieve an even rug.

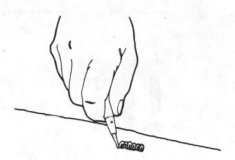

Make a chain stitch of loops. Skipping every two meshes will pack the loops tightly and keep them in place.

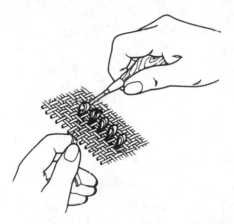

When beginning a new strip, start in the same hole as the finished strip. These two end cuts equal a full loop and do not create a hole in your work.

III

Color

Deciding upon our chosen design, whether hand drawn or adapted from a pattern, we have made the first commitment necessary in rug making. Now we must determine color. Color is the most significant attribute of a hooked rug. How many times have I seen a great design ruined by hideous colors!

Planning a rug may seem endless to an impatient beginner, but this is the part of rug making that I enjoy most. If you spend this time wisely and do not gloss over color decisions, you will never have to rip—what I enjoy doing least.

For those of you who are first venturing into color theory, take heart. I have taught it in third grade art classes, and they all got it.

The Color Wheel

To formulate a pleasing color scheme, we must become familiar with the color wheel. There are three primary colors: red, yellow, and blue, which make all the other colors of the spectrum. Red, yellow, and blue cannot be created but are basic hues. Orange, green, and purple (or violet) are secondary colors derived from combining the adjacent primary colors. Yellow and red make orange. Yellow and blue make green. Red and blue make violet.

Colors opposite from each other on the color wheel are called complements or opposites. Red and green (opposites) clash when placed side by side and set up a visual throb—the basic theory of Impressionist art. Orange and blue, and yellow and violet both create the same pulsing effect when placed side by side. Try taking some crayons in the six basic colors and color in the appropriate wedges on the color wheel for future reference. In this way you can see the colors and their relationships to one another.

Color schemes can be basically warm (hot colors: red, yellow, and orange) or cool (cold colors: blue, green, and purple). Neutrals are black, brown, tan, gray, and white. They are not actually colors, as they are not found in the spectrum, but they are shades and will be used in all rugs. Neutrals are found in the center of the color wheel because they are created by mixing complements or all the colors together. A grain or two of a dye will dull or dim its complement, much as adding gray or tan would do. Adding a few grains of red dye to bright green, for instance, will bring it down to a duller shade of green. This process is tricky. Be very cautious and add only a tiny amount.

Good color schemes are toned to warm or cool tones. Go to a fabric or upholstery center and look at the gorgeous printed fabrics available for draperies and slipcovers. This material has color registration marks at each selvage that show the exact colors used to print and overprint the fabric. You can see from the small blocks of color that a tone of color (warm or cool) was used. Compare two different color versions of the same print. Can you see how the greens vary from a warm color (adding more yellow to the dye) to a cool color (adding more blue to the dye)? When dyeing secondary colors for a color scheme, add more hot color to create a warm color scheme or more cold color to create a cool color scheme. Examples: yellow-green is a warm green, blue-green is a cool green.

Planning the Colors

Primitive rugs do not use brilliant modern colors. Bright reds, violent purples, turquoises, oranges, and acid greens have no place in old-looking rugs. Antique colors were made with natural dyes that were soft and muted and which faded with time. Harsh colors jump out of a rug and ruin the otherwise antique effect you are trying to create. Colors can be dark and strong without being harsh or bright.

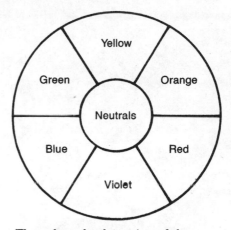

The color wheel consists of the primary colors, yellow, red, and blue, and the secondary colors, orange, violet, and green. Neutrals are placed in the center: black, brown, tan, gray, and white. These colors are made with opposites, or complementary colors on the color wheel.

Dyeing your own wool ensures a correct color. Colors achieved at home with Cushing dyes, no matter how deep the color, will never equal the intensity of those in commercially dyed fabrics.

Dyes

Natural Dyes

Until the midnineteenth century, all dyes were made from plant materials and, in some cases, animal sources. Red was originally derived from brazilwood, minerals, kermes grains, madder root, or cochineal (an insect found on cactus). The expensive cochineal was used to dye the scarlet coats of British soldiers; the cheaper madder root, less brilliant and apt to fade, was popular with farm folk.

Yellow was derived from sources as varied as sulfur, flowers, tree bark and roots, saffron pistils, and even dried onion skins. Used in combination with blue to form green and with red to form orange, yellow was an important dye.

Blue, an ancient dye, came primarily from the indigo plant. Because of its prevalence and availability from large indigo plantations, blue dye was the last chemical dye to be synthesized.

Natural dyes are not color- or light-fast. Sunlight dulls and dims them to the Colonial shades we cherish today. Originally, these colors and the resultant textiles were very bright. Turn over an old rug to see how bright the original colors were.

Mordants—chrome, copperas, tin, alum, and cream of tartar—were used in the dyeing process to gain different colors and shades from the same natural plant material. Logwood, a source of black dye, could be used with various mordants to achieve purple.

Neutral colors, such as black, brown, tan, and gray, were the most inexpensive and common dyes. They were made from bark, husks, and shells easily available on the farm. Confederate uniforms were dyed a butternut with walnut shells and husks. This color of Confederate homespun gradually replaced the gray of manufactured goods as the Civil War wore on.

Making Brown Dye from Walnuts

Black walnut shells, saved after the nutmeats are removed, are an excellent source of strong brown dye. They are clean and can be stored for years. A handful of walnut shells soaked overnight and simmered several hours produces a lovely bone tint that can be used to dull and age bright colors. So save nutshells, particularly black walnuts, to make a dye solution to "dirty" bright wool and dim white wool to an antique white.

I gather walnut husks (those inky outer shells) in the autumn when they fall off the trees. No matter how rotten and stinky (also worm-ridden) they are, they produce a lovely brown dye. Cook walnut husks outside. I use an electric hot plate on a card table in the driveway or use the gas grill. The smell is awful, and if the dye was cooked inside, the house would be redolent of dirty sweat socks! After soaking the husks for twenty-four hours one day and simmering them for eight, I strain off the broth and bottle it for future use. Some of my walnut dye turns moldy in the jar (stored on shelves in the garage), but I just strain off the gunk and use the dye. It retains its color (and the smell). The original full-strength brew of these black walnuts produces a wonderful warm brown unobtainable with any other dye and results in the authentic walnut brown of antique textiles.

A cupful of black walnut dye in 4 quarts of water, plus 1 tablespoon of salt and ½ cup of white vinegar, will lend a lovely bone color to white wool and dull bright colors. Test your new bone tint with a scrap of the wool you plan to age before immersing the whole piece. Walnut is one dye that does not need to mature in the dye bath, so remove your stained piece when the color is what you want. Remember that wet wool is always darker than dry wool. Wash the piece in a mild detergent, rinse, and dry. You have aged your wool with nature's bounty.

Aniline Dyes

Chemical dyes, known as aniline, were first synthesized from coal tar in England. Aniline purple was named mauve when introduced as a dye in 1856. Magenta followed in 1859, then Hofman violet (1863) and Britannia violet (1865). All these vivid purples outraged staid England. This rejection of the new chemical colors caused a fall in prosperity of the dyeing trade. With the reluctance of English firms to convert to anilines, the industry moved to Germany. Chemical dyeing required new processes for its application, outmoding the ancient dyeing industry in England.

In Germany new colors flooded the market: alizarin scarlet (1870), green (1877), naphthol yellow (1886), and artificial blue (1890) with infinite combinations of these colors. To the late nineteenth century, these Berlin colors were a wonder. At last, brilliant colors were available to people at affordable prices. Thus the bright and often garish colors of the Victorian era began.

The 1880s saw an explosion of color. Textile companies leaped to make the new and highly salable fabrics and yarns. The demand for the new vivid colors was insatiable. Scottish cotton mills were the last to make the conversion from natural to aniline dyes. This was a sizable investment and one that demanded more chemical colors to replace those formerly made with natural dyes. Fortunes were made and lost in the next two decades. The elusive blue was the last to be synthesized, in 1890, causing the Indigo Panic of 1910. Indigo planters refused to acknowledge the importance of chemical dyeing and clung to an outmoded industry.

Country women rushed to buy the new goods. Saving money and countless hours of precious working time, they could now purchase the printed calicos and brilliant solid colors. Even the Amish people of Lancaster County established a tradition of bright colors for shirts and dresses, tempered by black aprons, shawls, and suits. Their bishops accepted the new color choices in piece goods as a labor-saving device, making the bought fabric with its brilliant colors acceptable to the Amish community.

Dulling or Removing Color

When I first began rug hooking with that fabulous collection of saved wools, I had a great variety of bright colors. To use them for primitives, I had to dull or remove some color for the antique effect I desired. Remembering the color wheel, I added a few grains of dye of the opposite (or complementary) color to dull or tone down bright colors. This method is tricky and experimental, but only a few grains are necessary to dim garish colors. Too much will dull the color to mud and be very dismal.

Another method of dulling or color removal is simmering the bright color in a mild detergent. One squirt to a quart is sufficient to start. Continue draining off the bubbling, colored water and adding fresh water. Keep your eye on the resultant color. Wool can often bleed out quickly and become too light. On the other hand, sometimes no dye leaches out, and stronger measures are called for. Adding one teaspoon of non-sudsy ammonia to the detergent water can occasionally do the trick but is a last resort, as ammonia weakens wool. Never, and I mean never, use chlorine bleach on wool.

You can also soften the offending color with a dip dye of walnut, tea, or coffee. These natural dyes—never black—can dirty a bright color to a pleasant shade. I use weak walnut dye for dyeing bone and tan and dulling many colors. It is a strong and permanent dye.

PATTERN

"Little Holstein"

16½ by 26½ inches

MATERIALS

Cow

White body. 4 ounces or ⅓ yard of white wool flannel.
Black spots. 4 ounces or ⅓ yard of black wool flannel.
Eyes and nostrils. Scrap of medium brown wool.
Horns. Scrap of gold wool.
Hair tuft. Scrap of off-white wool.
Udder. ½ ounce of pale pink wool.
Hooves. Scraps of black-and-white checked wool.

Background

8 ounces of white wool to dye Reseda Green or shades of green.

Border

4 ounces of Egyptian Red or barn red wool.
4 ounces of green checked wool or black-and-white checked
wool to dye Reseda Green.

Outside edge

3 ounces of dark green wool.

DYES
(W. Cushing & Co.)

Reseda Green
Egyptian Red

Dyeing for "Little Holstein"

Always start with the background color. Middle-tone backgrounds are the most difficult to work with, as many colors disappear on them. Begin with a light background or dark background; your center of interest will contrast with the chosen background color.

Our first pattern, "Little Holstein," is black and white. These colors are opposite ends of the neutral spectrum. Against black and white, any middle tone will look good. I chose Reseda Green, but country blue or barn red would be good choices, too. I also make a Guernsey cow rug using natural dyes with this pattern, choosing rust and white for the cow and a khaki (army blanket) background.

If you lay out the material for the background, folded four times, and place your black-and-white fabric on it, you can tell immediately if the cow will stand out. By the way—never outline a primitive subject with a dark color. If you did not plan ahead and your subject is lost against the background, do not resort to a harsh outline.

Dyeing the Background

Follow the general dyeing information in section II for dyeing the background. Presoak the 8-ounce piece of white wool and simmer the dye bath (³/₃₂ teaspoon of Reseda Green plus 1 tablespoon of salt). Immerse the wool, lifting it once or twice to expose all of it to the dye. By crowding the wool in the dye pot and not stirring or lifting it again, you will create a nice mottled effect. In half an hour all the dye should be taken up. Permit the wool to cool in the dye bath until it is warm. See section II for directions on washing, rinsing, and drying the wool.

Dyeing the Border

The border for "Little Holstein" is a simple block design using 4 ounces each of red wool and green checked wool. Smaller amounts of wool can be utilized for each block of color if you wish to use a number of different colors in your border blocks. My color scheme, however, calls for alternating blocks of red and green wool. There are thirty-eight blocks (nineteen of each color), with thirteen top and bottom (twenty-six) and six on each side. The uneven number—nineteen—allows me to center a block. But it doesn't really matter if the blocks don't work out numerically. This is a primitive rug, remember.

I like to color-key the border to blend with the background and achieve an overall look. If you have to dye the green-and-black checks, use four ounces of black-and-white checked wool (⅓ yard). Dissolve $^2/_{32}$ teaspoon of Reseda Green plus 1 teaspoon of salt in a 1-gallon pan of water filled three-quarters full. Simmer the dye solution. Presoak the checked wool and drop it into the dye bath. Stir and lift to expose all the wool to the dye, cover, and simmer for half an hour. Wash, rinse, and dry the wool.

To dye the alternate border blocks red, presoak ⅓ yard or 4 ounces of white wool. Dissolve $^4/_{32}$ teaspoon of Egyptian Red in a 1-gallon dye pot filled three-quarters full. Add 1 teaspoon of salt and simmer until the dye is dissolved. Drop in the white wool, stir and lift to expose all the fabric to the dye, cover, and simmer for half an hour. Wash, rinse, and dry the wool.

You can use the background color for the two-row border edge or use dark green wool, as I do. Three ounces will be required.

Hooking "Little Holstein"

Before beginning to hook your rug, see "Cutting the Wool" in section II. I will be using only #8 (¼-inch) strips for this pattern.

Hooking the Cow

Start with small details in the center of the rug: eyes, nostrils, hair tuft, and horns. I like to start hooking an animal with the face. Hook the brown eyes, the sides of the face, and the white nose. Follow with udder and hooves before moving along to the body.

When beginning the larger areas, always outline first, then fill in the area. Although I usually suggest outlining the animal first, in this case you cannot because of the spots. Start with the black spots, outlining before hooking into the center; then outline the outside edge of the cow with white where indicated before finishing the rest of the body. I like to hook in the direction the body parts indicate—curved for pig's ribs, contoured for cow's spots. Working from the center of the rug out to the sides keeps the tension expanding and results in a flat rug. Fill in the subject before beginning the background.

Hooking the Background

For the background, I like to use undulating directional hooking, but you can also do straight lines if you wish (see section IV, "Line and Directional Hooking.") Wavy directional hooking contrasts nicely with the straight hooking of the border blocks, creating an interesting textural effect. To plan your background hooking, make directional lines or dashes on your foundation with a permanent marking pen after you have traced your pattern. The dashes will remind you where to go.

Begin the background by outlining one row of the background color around the cow and another row around the border to provide a place to turn when bumping up against the edges. Then begin to strike a wave or to hook in a straight line. Never cut off the strips as they hit the sides of the rug, but turn around and finish the strips somewhere in the field, changing the location of the cut ends so they do not pile up in one place. If you don't, you will create an unsightly line of cut ends running down the edge of your rug. You must learn to reverse directions at the edge and hook back into the field before cutting your strip, scattering the ends through the rug so that they are barely visible. Hooking with long strips limits the number of cut ends.

Hook your initials somewhere in the field. In a corner or in the border blocks is a good place to identify your work.

If this is a cow you have known and loved, her name could be included in the border blocks using one block per letter, providing the spelling does not exceed thirteen letters!

Hooking the Border

Having completed the center of the rug and finished the background, we must now hook the border blocks. Always alternate the direction of each block in a basket-weave fashion. I make directional notations on each block, varying the direction in every other block. By doing this, your rug will lie flat and not ripple at the edges.

Hook your two outside rows before beginning the blocks. You need a straight line to bump up against to keep the blocks square. It is also important to hook two consecutive rows at the outer edges of any rug to save the design in case of damage to the edges, always the first place to wear. If you plan to alternate red and green-checked squares as I have done, start in one corner and hook each block in order. If you plan to use up little scraps of various colored wools for the border blocks, use a color sequence that alternates light and dark colors for a balanced border appearance. I have seen the "Little Holstein" border hooked with a variety of colors and patterns, and it is very cheerful—and economical. What a great place to use up scraps!

Finishing Your Rug

To finish a rug, country women merely turned over the outside edges of the burlap and hooked these edges into the body of the rug. Disaster! When the rug begins to wear, the edges go first, along with the border design. You can see attempts to repair the worn edges with cotton binding on many old rugs. I bind the rug with overcast wool yarn before adding the cotton rug tape to ensure survival. For complete instructions on binding the finished rug, see section VIII, "Hemming Your Rug."

PATTERN ——————————————————————————————

"Little Guernsey"

16½ by 26½ inches

© Pat Hornafius 1990

M A T E R I A L S ————————————————————————

Cow

Rust body. 4 ounces of rust wool or wool dyed with onion skin.
Brown Rust dye can be used if you aren't using natural dye.
White spots. 4 ounces of white wool.
Eyes and nostrils. Scrap of black wool.
Hooves. Scrap of black-and-white checked wool.
Hair tuft. Scrap of off-white wool.
Udder. ½ ounce of pale pink or pale goldenrod spotted with very
light Terra Cotta.
Horns. Scrap of deep goldenrod or marigold or Old Gold.

Background and two outside rows

12 ounces of dark khaki wool overdyed with Dark Green.

Border

2 ounces of wool dyed Terra Cotta.
4 ounces of wool dyed marigold or goldenrod or Old Gold, torn
in 1-ounce strips.
4 ounces of wool dyed with onion skin or Brown Rust, torn in 1-
ounce strips.

D Y E S ————————
(W. Cushing & Co.)

Brown Rust (or natural onion skins)

**Old Gold (or goldenrod or marigold
natural dyes)**

Dark Green

Terra Cotta

Dyeing for "Little Guernsey"

If you wish to use natural dyes, turning "Little Holstein" into "Little Guernsey" is the perfect choice.

I use Golden Globe dried onion skins for the rust cow color. Gather these shells all year long from the onion bin at your local market. My grocer saves them for me at no cost, but I've been known to tidy the onion department myself to the customers' amazement and the manager's delight!

Following the directions for "Little Holstein," I substitute black eyes for the Guernsey and make rust spots on the cow rather than black ones.

Dyeing the Background

For the background, I like to use a khaki army-blanket color overdyed with $1/32$ teaspoon of Dark Green in 2 cups of boiling water plus 1 tablespoon of white vinegar. Presoak the khaki wool and scrunch it in a kettle with about 1 or 2 inches of water. You do not want to dye the entire piece, just diffuse darker green spots over the top of the wool. The diluted solution will not create definite spots (which you don't want), but it will gently blend into the body of the wool, creating a softly mottled appearance in the background. See section II for directions on washing, rinsing, and drying the wool.

"Half and Half Dyeing" in section II describes another method of dyeing the "Little Guernsey" background using Dark Green and Khaki Drab for a stained-glass effect.

Dyeing the Cow and Border Blocks

Pack your onion shells in a 2-gallon kettle of water and simmer one hour. You will see the deep rust color leaching from the skins. Add 1 tablespoon of salt and ¼ cup of white vinegar and immerse the 4-ounce presoaked white wool piece and one of the 1-ounce strips directly into the onion skin dye bath. Simmer for one hour. This procedure will give you the deepest value possible with onion skins for the cow's spots and two blocks of the border.

A half hour after immersing the first 1-ounce strip, immerse the second strip. Simmer this strip for the remaining half hour along with the first one. The second strip will be a medium rust shade.

Achieving light shades of rust from onion skins is a mess. You must strain out the shells and the wool from the dye bath. Pour the whole works into a colander suspended over another kettle. You can use cooking equipment, as onion skins are not poisonous.

Extricate the wool from the shells, and rinse it thoroughly. Be careful not to put these spent shells down the garbage disposal. I did and paid a huge plumbing bill to unplug the pipes. Clean the onion shells off the wool by running warm tap water over the strips before washing them in mild detergent.

You now have the second dye bath of paler onion water in your second kettle. Add 1 tablespoon of vinegar to increase take-up, and simmer the third strip for half an hour in the bath. Add the fourth and final strip after half an hour and 1 more tablespoon of vinegar to absorb all the dye.

You should have four shades of rust when your onion dye is spent. Wash, rinse, and dry your wool.

If you are using Brown Rust dye to get the rust wool needed for the cow and border, use $2/32$ teaspoon for 4 ounces of white wool and follow the directions below for substituting Old Gold dye.

Dyeing the Rest of the Border

I like to make my border blocks various shades of onion and goldenrod or marigold natural dye. If you do not care to use these flowers for the soft gold tones, substitute Old Gold Cushing dye.

Goldenrod as a dye. In August when the yellow blossoms are at their peak, pinch the heads and simmer them in a large kettle of water for several hours. This is not a bright dye but a lovely soft golden-tan. If you include the green leaves and stems of the goldenrod, the dye will have a yellow-green cast. Proceed with dyeing the four 1-ounce wool strips as you did with the onion shells, adding 1 tablespoon of salt and ¼ cup of white vinegar to the initial dye bath. Permit the wool to cool in the dye bath for complete take-up. Wash, rinse, and dry the wool.

Marigolds as a dye. In early September when yellow (not mixed or rust) marigolds are at their peak, pluck enough flower heads to fill a gallon bucket, simmer them for several hours, and dye one or two strips for the border. This yellow is lighter and brighter than goldenrod dye, but it blends beautifully in the border with the rust shades. Use 1 tablespoon of salt and ¼ cup of white vinegar as mordants in the initial dye bath. Natural dyes have a very slow take-up, so permit the wool to cool in the dye bath. Wash, rinse, and dry the wool.

Both goldenrod and marigold dye will keep in a jar, but with age the color will dim.

Substituting Old Gold dye. If you do not have access to flowers or the desire to use them for your yellow dye, substitute Old Gold dye. Dye four 1-ounce strips of white wool sequentially in $2/32$ teaspoon of Old Gold to two quarts of water plus 1 tablespoon of salt. The salt will retard the take-up, so you can achieve four shades of gold.

Darkest: Immerse one strip and count to fifteen.

Medium: Immerse the next strip and count to fifteen.

Light: Immerse the next strip and count to fifteen.

Very light: Immerse the last strip and count to fifteen. Add 1 teaspoon of vinegar, stir thoroughly, and simmer all the strips for half an hour. Wash the wool, rinse, and let it dry. You will have four shades of gold.

Plan to alternate the gold and rust shades in the border blocks and place the darkest rust color in the top center and the bottom center of the row of blocks. Alternate the gold and rust blocks in a light-dark pattern to distribute the values around the border.

I like to hook a separation row of background color between the rust and gold blocks. It helps to define the soft, natural dye colors.

Dyeing the Terra-cotta Corners

Terra-cotta corners are dyed with $4/32$ teaspoon of Terra Cotta to 2 ounces of white wool. Add the dye plus 1 teaspoon of salt to 1 quart of water. You can also overdye a beige, tan, or off-white piece for these corner blocks, as the terra cotta is a deep color. Simmer the dye solution and add the wool. Simmer fifteen minutes, add 1 tablespoon of white vinegar, and continue to simmer fifteen minutes more. The vinegar is necessary for take-up. Wash, rinse, and dry the wool.

Dyeing the Udder

You need ½ ounce of pink wool for the udder. If you would rather dye the udder, use ½ ounce of palest goldenrod or palest Old Gold–dyed wool. Before immersing the material for the corner blocks, save 1 tablespoon of simmered Terra Cotta dye. Place the small presoaked piece of udder fabric in a small pan. On the wet palest-gold wool, sprinkle several spots of hot Terra Cotta dye. These spots will diffuse into the wet pale-gold wool and give an interesting tone of pinky-gold to the udder. To set the dye, add a scant ¼ inch of water, if needed, and cover, simmer, and turn off the heat. Permit the wool to cool in the pan. The pan must not boil dry, but the steam will set the red spots. Wash, rinse, and dry the wool.

Hooking "Little Guernsey"

Before beginning to hook your rug, see the directions on cutting the wool in section II. You can hook "Little Guernsey" by following the hooking directions for "Little Holstein."

PATTERN

"Pat's Pig"

33 by 23 inches

MATERIALS

Pink Pig

8 ounces of white wool to dye or ⅔ yard of pink wool.
3 shades of darker pink for various parts of the pig (ears, teats, right legs, snout, underbelly, tail, and border lines).
6 ounces of white wool to dye or ½ yard of dark pink wool.

Background

16 ounces of white wool or 1⅓ yards of green wool.

Border

4 ounces of dark green wool.

Grass

4 ounces of several darker green wools.

Details

Scraps of white, black, camel, gold, and yellow-green wool.

DYES
(W. Cushing & Co.)

Peacock

Reseda Green

Egyptian Red

Mummy Brown

Dark Green

Nugget Gold

Changing the Rug Size or Breed of Pig

"Pat's Pig" is an easy beginner rug that can be enlarged by the addition of a more interesting border (see section V for border designs). Because of the simplicity of the pig's shape, a more complex border would enhance the design of the rug. Conversely, to make a smaller version of "Pat's Pig," eliminate the grass plot and daisies.

If you wish to change the type of pig, use an encyclopedia or book on swine for breed characteristics. I have made this rug using several pig variations by adding spots (Spotted pig) or a neck stripe (the Hampshire breed). The basic shape remains the same.

In designing the spotted pig rug, I simplified the field, removing grass and daisies, and complicated the border. The black-and-white checks repeat the color of the pig, and I mottled an ochre background with Old Gold and Golden Brown dye.

Dyeing for "Pat's Pig"

"Pat's Pig" has a simple color scheme—shades of pink and green, plus scraps of black, white, camel, gold, and yellow-green. Because of the simplicity of the design, mottled dyeing makes this rug interesting. The variations in the background color and subtle mottling of the pink pig add interest to an otherwise flat design.

Dyeing the Background

"Pat's Pig" takes 16 ounces or 1⅓ yards of white wool for the background. Always presoak the wool in warm water for half an hour before immersing it in the hot dye bath. Presoaking opens the fibers for accepting the dye. If your water is extremely hard or your wool contains a synthetic fiber, a few drops of mild liquid detergent or a few grains of water softener will make take-up easier.

For a rug 33 by 23 inches, you will need ¼ teaspoon of Reseda Green and ¼ teaspoon of Peacock to dye the wool for the background, the border, and the grass. Combine and dissolve both dyes in 2 cups of boiling water. You will use ½ of this solution for dyeing the 16 ounces of white wool for the background and the other half for dyeing the 8 ounces of wool for the darker border and the grass.

Fill a 2-gallon kettle three-quarters full of water and add 1 cup of dye solution along with 1 tablespoon of plain salt. Heat this dye bath until it is simmering. Stir thoroughly before immersing the 16 ounces of background wool. When immersing the wool, crowd it into the pot. Lift once or twice to be sure all surfaces of the wool have received the dye, then crowd it back into the kettle and permit it to simmer for half an hour. If you continually lift the wool or keep stirring it, the dye will be evenly distributed and your wool will not be mottled. You want it mottled.

After fifteen minutes, add ¼ cup of white vinegar and stir rapidly once. If you had added vinegar to the initial dye bath, you would have gotten a very rapid take-up that results in a variegated dye, from white to dark green. This effect is wonderful for leaves or small areas, but I prefer a more subtle range of color tones for a background color.

If you wish darker areas and more variegation, add additional dye of $1/_{32}$ teaspoon of Reseda Green in 1 cup of boiling water and puddle it on top of the simmering wool crowded in the pan. This process is called spot dyeing. The areas that receive the additional dye will be darker, so don't stir the dye this time or you will dissolve your spots. See section II for directions on washing, rinsing, and drying the wool.

Dyeing the Border and the Grass
Use the remaining cup of Reseda Green and Peacock dye solution to dye the dark green border material (4 ounces) and the grass (4 ounces). Heat a 1-gallon kettle of water, add the 1 cup

of dye solution plus 1 tablespoon of salt, and simmer. Immerse the presoaked wool strips, stirring thoroughly to expose all the surfaces to the dye. Add ¼ cup of vinegar after fifteen minutes and continue to simmer for half an hour. Wash, rinse, and dry the wool.

You may use plain white wool for these areas or combine neutral checks, plaids, and stripes for a more interesting and varied texture for the grass. If you are using plain wool (4 ounces) for the grass, you will need to mottle it with other colors. After the original dye bath is completed, remove the wet wool for the grass plot and fold it accordionlike in a foil-lined baking dish. Do not wash or rinse it. Drain off the excess water. Dissolve 1/64 teaspoon of Nugget Gold and 1/64 teaspoon of Dark Green in separate measuring cups. Add 1 cup of boiling water to each. Pour alternate rows of hot yellow and dark green dye onto the folded material, skipping a space between rows. This solution does not need more salt or vinegar, as the mordants are still in the unwashed wool. Cover the pan with foil and heat gently in the oven (200 degrees F.) or on top of the stove for half an hour. Be sure the pan does not become dry. Wash, rinse, and dry the wool.

Dyeing the Pig

To dye the pig pink, use 8 ounces of white wool and 6 ounces more for the darker pinks needed for the ears, snout, teats, tail, underbelly, right legs, and border lines. Rip the 6-ounce piece into three strips for the varying shades for the accents.

You can dye all these shades in the same dye bath by placing them in the dye pot in consecutive order, darkest pink (legs) to lightest pink (body of the pig).

Dissolve 1/32 teaspoon of Egyptian Red and 1/64 teaspoon of Mummy Brown in 1 cup of hot water, and add it to a simmering 2-gallon pot ¾ full of water. Add 2 teaspoons of salt and simmer until all the particles are dissolved.

Plan to dye in this order:

1. Darkest. Right legs, ear outline, back ear, and teats (2-ounce strip).

2. Medium. Snout, tail, and underbelly (2-ounce strip).

3. Lightest. Border lines and front ear (2-ounce strip).

4. Pig. 8 ounces of white wool.

When the dye bath is ready, immerse the presoaked strips one at a time, counting to fifteen between consecutive immersions. The salt will retard fast take-up so that when you finally drop in the 8 ounces of white wool for the pig, the color will be pale but still pink enough to make a pleasant shade of pig pink. Crowd the 8-ounce piece in the pan, cover, and simmer all your pig wool for half an hour. Spin out, wash, rinse, and dry the wool.

Dyeing the Details

The scraps of white, black, camel, gold, and yellow-green are for the smallest areas in the pig rug.

White. Daisy petals.

Black. Nostril, eye, mouth.

Camel. Hooves, lines in snout, one line under the ear, one line behind each leg.

Gold. Daisy centers.

Shades of yellow-green. Daisy stems and leaves.

Egyptian Red overdyed on tan wool. Tip of snout and line under mouth.

The tiny amount of gold needed for the daisy centers (three strands) can be dyed with Nugget Gold. Dissolve $1/32$ teaspoon of Nugget Gold dye in 1 cup of boiling water plus $1/4$ teaspoon of salt. Cover and simmer for five minutes. Wash, rinse, and dry the wool.

Combining Nugget Gold and Reseda Green will create your yellow-green for leaves and stems—use 1 ounce of white wool dyed with $1/64$ teaspoon of Reseda Green and $1/32$ teaspoon of Nugget Gold. Add 2 teaspoons of vinegar to the initial dye bath to mottle the colors. Cover and simmer fifteen minutes. Wash, rinse, and dry the wool. Another way to get yellow-green for the leaves and stems is to overdye the yellow material you already have for the daisy centers (about $1/2$ ounce) with $1/64$ teaspoon of Reseda Green. Presoak the yellow wool. Dissolve and simmer the Reseda Green dye in 1 quart of water. Immerse the yellow wool and simmer for fifteen minutes. Wash, rinse, and dry the wool.

The tip of the pig's snout should be the darkest pink you have. I use a camel strip overdyed with $1/64$ teaspoon of Egyptian Red in 1 cup of boiling water for this area and for the line under the mouth. Dissolve the dye plus ½ teaspoon of salt in 1 cup of water. Immerse the strip and simmer for five minutes. Wash, rinse, and dry the wool.

I am assuming that you have scraps of white, black, and camel wool for the first three details numbered above. Of course, if you don't wish to dye details 4, 5, and 6, you can find wool in these colors.

Hooking "Pat's Pig"

Before beginning to hook your rug, see "Cutting the Wool" in section II.

Hooking the Pig

Begin with the smallest areas as enumerated in "Dyeing the Details." Then start with the pig and make the black eye, nostril, and mouth. Hook in the tip of the pig's snout with the camel strip you overdyed with Egyptian Red. Hook in the face lines with the darkest pink (see #1, under "Dyeing the Pig") and the snout lines with camel, and hook one row of camel under the ear to create a shadow. I outline the ear and cheek with one row of darkest pink and then outline the legs and hook the teats.

The right legs, one row in the tail, the underbelly, and the rear ear are the next darkest pink (#2). Use some #2 pink for the underchin and more rows of pink in the snout. I like to use this shade for one row inside the forward ear and then fill in the rest of the ear with #3 pink for a gradual shading.

No. 3 pink is used for the front ear and border lines. Make a second row with #4 pink to complete the tail.

After completing the face details, finish the head in #4 pink. Outline the body parts and then follow the contour of the ribs. I hook several rows of pig pink over the back of my pig before beginning to contour the body.

Hooking the Grass and Your Initials

If you have not done so already, hook the flowers and hooves and move on to the grass plot, your initials and the date. Always sign your work with your initials. I date my rugs as well. Identifying your work of art is as important as signing a painting. You are painting in wool, and future generations will remember your work in this way.

Hooking the Background

Outline the pig and the grass plot with your background color. Use a permanent marking pen to dash in directional lines to indicate wavy hooking, and hook one row around the border with pink to outline the background. You need a line to bump up against when you turn your rows. Do not cut off each row as it touches the border edge. Turn around and hook back into the field before ending the strip. Follow the undulating waves drawn in with your permanent marking pen and fill in the background.

Hooking the Border

You have already hooked one row of pink at the edge of the background. Now using the dark green wool, hook four rows at the edge of the rug and finish with one row of pink. See section VIII for directions on hemming your rug.

IV

Line and Directional Hooking

When you are hooking, you are creating a line—a row of loops. The direction in which you move these rows creates variety, movement, and vigor within the rug. The interplay of light and shadow on the surface of the rug contributes to this visual texture.

As stated earlier, the type of hooking frame used can determine the hooking style for the background. The small opening in a sawbuck-type frame hampers creativity in curves and wavy backgrounds because the hooker can only see 12 inches at a time. Quilt-type frames, which leave more space open to the hooker's eye, accommodate more active fields. Primitive art favors straight-line hooking, simplistic and rigid. More sophisticated treatments reveal undulating background rows.

Straight-Line Hooking

Hooking in a straight line gives a rigidity to hooking that can be very interesting if handled in an imaginative way, such as hit-and-miss. Hit-and-miss is a method by which the background or border is hooked with different colored strips used in sequence. This method creates a sense of vigor in the rug. Using strips from the last of the ragbag, inventive rugmakers filled in backgrounds with whatever color their hand chose. Called hit-and-miss, these fields created movement by the hooking direction of the strips and the varying colors.

Hit-and-miss was the place to use up leftovers. Since a

large quantity of one color necessary for backgrounds was often unavailable, hit-and-miss was a favorite with country rugmakers.

Hit-and-Miss Backgrounds

When using a hit-and-miss background, keep the subject matter simple. Plain colors work best in the foreground or the center of interest. "Six Hearts and Miss" is a perfect example of a simple subject and variegated background. The six hearts are Terra Cotta red. The background is a variety of hit-and-miss colors. Limit your background choices to basically neutral wools—tweeds, checks, beige, taupe, and one dark color (navy, brown, or dark green)—to outline the blocks and hook the two rows in the border. This one color can set the color tone of the rug for an overall appearance. Overdye some of the lightest shades of neutrals (plaids, checks, stripes) in a weak dye bath of the chosen accent color to tie together the accumulation of varying fabrics.

Color Choices for Hit-and-Miss

Planning a hit-and-miss rug takes time. Although the color selection seems casual, you must ensure that the colors and fabrics are evenly spaced over the surface of the rug. To avoid running out of a particular wool, I evenly divide my amounts— six sections in the case of "Six Hearts and Miss"—as I'm cutting the background, putting an equal amount of strips in separate piles before moving on to the next color. In this way, I can plan for the proper amount for each section and not run short.

Speaking of short, do not use strips less than 6 inches long. Hit-and-miss is a great way to use up snippets, but tiny pieces can weaken any rug. If using yard goods for hit-and-miss, cut your 4-inch torn strips into thirds (about 20 inches long) before cutting ¼-inch strips. This length works up as a nice line of color without taking over an entire section. Of course, shorter strips from remnants and ripped clothing also work. Varying the length of the strips adds interest to the field. Long and short strips should be alternated.

For the hit-and-miss backgrounds, I like to plan my colors to include equal amounts of light, medium, and dark wools. Use beige, off-white, cream, or light colors for your lightest colors in the rug, never white. Medium tones include taupe, camel, tan, soft-colored tweeds, plaids, and checks. Some of these pale colors can be overdyed in the color used in the border (the color that sets the tone of the rug). For your dark tones, use dark plaids, checks, or tweeds predominantly in the border color or overdyed in that hue.

When determining the quantity of wool needed for a hit-and-miss background, multiply the area to be covered by four and divide that weight or amount by three (light, medium, and dark wools). Throw in a little extra of the value that will predominate. A light-appearing rug needs more pale colors, a darker background more somber shades.

Hit-and-Miss in Antique Rugs

Old hit-and-miss rugs were often wild. Everything went into the background—wool, cotton, silk, knit stockings, and long underwear, all in multicolored hues. Often these have been the most vigorous rugs I have encountered. An antique "Two Dog" design creates the wagging of tails by the use of a slight rise and fall in directional hooking behind the tails. The jog in the hit-and-miss hooking creates a feeling of movement in an otherwise static horizontal field. A running horse becomes a fiery steed when hooked with multicolored strips—red predominating in an undulating hooking pattern. A simple red star stands out in a sky of zigzag hit-and-miss fireworks. All these effects were unintentional, I'm sure, but using a grabbag background enlivened a simple subject, making it a museum piece.

"Little Guernsey"

"Pat's Pig"

"Six Hearts and Miss"

"Spot"

"Pat's Swan"

"Boston Baked Beans"

BOSTON BAKED BEANS

"Renfrew Cats"

"Puppy with Targets"

"Rooster with Rabbit Cart"

"Doves with Pansies"

"Little Lamb Pulltoy"

"Nesting Chickens"

"American Trotter"

"Antique Flower Basket"

"American Fruit Piece"

PATTERN ————————————————————————————

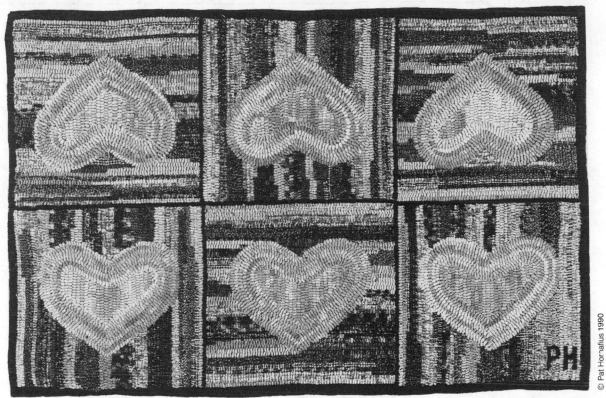

© Pat Hornafius 1990

"Six Hearts and Miss"

25 by 37 inches

© Pat Hornafius 1990

DYES
(W. Cushing & Co.)

Terra Cotta

Dark Brown, Dark Green, or Navy if needed

MATERIALS

Hearts

12 ounces of white wool or 1 yard of red wool.

Border and block outlines

4 ounces of any dark color that will color-tone your hit-and-miss strips. I use dark green, but navy or brown work well.

Hit-and-miss blocks

A variety of neutrals, plaids, stripes, checks, and solids in tan, beige, taupe, and camel. Include some of the block-outline material plus lighter shades of that color. Use about 4 ounces of cut strips for each 12-inch square (six sections).

Drawing the Pattern

Plan the size of your blocks before cutting out the heart pattern. I have used an 8-inch heart for six 12-inch-square blocks. Section off the rug into six equal blocks, allowing ½ inch on each edge for two rows of border hooking.

Using a measuring square for straight corners, draw the outside dimensions (24 by 36 inches) on the burlap with a permanent marker. Add the ½-inch outside border for two rows of hooking. Section the rug into six blocks 12 inches square. Center your heart pattern in each block. The placement of the hearts will depend on where the rug will be seen. If it will be viewed from both directions, place tips outward. If seen from one side only, place the heart tips in the same direction.

Dyeing for "Six Hearts and Miss"

This rug uses odds and ends, but to obtain an overall color tone, you can tint some of the lightest plaids or checks with your border color. Dark Brown, Dark Green, or Navy dye is used to tint neutrals for your hit-and-miss blocks.

Dyeing the Hearts

Six hearts take 12 ounces of red wool. Because this is an antique design, use a mottled look of soft faded red.

I like to use Terra Cotta dye for the warm old red color. Egyptian Red works equally well here, but it is a cooler tone of red. Per ounce of white wool, use 1/32 teaspoon of Terra Cotta (or Egyptian Red) for a medium shade (for 12 ounces, ¼ teaspoon plus 4/32 teaspoon of dye). Dissolve the dye with 1 tablespoon of salt in a 2-gallon dye pot filled three-quarters full of water. Simmer the dye bath to be sure all particles are dissolved before adding the presoaked wool. Lift the wet wool once or twice to be sure all surfaces have touched the dye solution before scrunching the wool into the dye pot. You want a mottled look here. See section II for directions on washing, rinsing, and drying the wool.

Dyeing the Background

Your border color and cross stripes set the color tone for your rug. Accumulate your wools first before determining the border color, the deepest hue. Throw all your neutrals—tweeds, checks, plaids—on the floor and see what tone predominates. I have used dark green, navy, or brown in this rug design for three completely different but equally beautiful rugs. Whatever dark color will enhance your accumulated background colors is the right choice. If in doubt, lay a piece of the intended border wool on top of the pile. Does it blend? If any of the neutrals need a hint of the border color to enliven your rug, you can tint this amount.

I frequently use a weak solution of the dominant color to tie in fabrics that are too clean or white for the overall look. Depending on the amount of wool to be tinted, add a few grains per ounce in a small dye pot. A very light touch is all you want. Add ½ teaspoon of salt to the dye bath. Simmer the dye to dissolve the particles, and test the color with a selvage or bias piece (from used clothing). If the dye is too dark, remove some of the solution for later use and add more water. If it is too light, a few more grains of dye will do.

Remembering your complements from the color wheel, dull bright fabrics to make them compatible with your background. Use a grain or two of the complementary dye color to dim the wool in a very weak dye bath (add ¼ teaspoon of salt). Be cautious: Too much dye will blank out the original color, leaving gray or mud.

Having chosen your border color, you may not need to dye any wool. If you want to dye this dark border color, you can overdye a gray, beige, taupe, or other neutral light to medium wool.

Use $^{2}/_{32}$ teaspoon of the chosen color per ounce or ¼ teaspoon for the 4 ounces. It is a heavy load of dye for such a small piece, so plan to add 1 teaspoon of salt to start and ¼ cup of vinegar after simmering fifteen minutes. Continue simmering for half an hour. Permit the wool to cool in the dye bath to complete the take-up.

Wash, rinse, and dry the wool.

Hooking "Six Hearts and Miss"

Before beginning to hook your rug, see "Cutting the Wool" in section II.

Hooking the Hearts

Hook the hearts first. Outline, then continue with four more contouring rows before changing to straight hooking. If you continue to outline in a curve into the middle of the heart, the center will pop out and not lie flat.

Hooking the Field

Don't forget to hook in your initials and the date in a corner of the rug before filling in the field.

Using your darker accent tone, hook the lines dividing the blocks and the innermost border row. With hit-and-miss hooking you need to bump against a row before reversing the strip.

If your rug is perfectly drawn on the straight of the burlap, each row will follow a row of meshes. Indicate a straight line every so often with a permanent magic marker. Keep your rows straight and do not follow the curve of the hearts, but hook to the edge and reverse the strip. Do not cut off each strip at the edge of the heart.

Complete each block and finish with another row or two of plain dark strips in the outside border to accommodate wear. Finish your rug using the directions given in section VIII, "Hemming Your Rug."

PATTERN

"Spot"

29 by 31 inches

MATERIALS

Dog

6 ounces of medium brown wool or white wool dyed with black walnut shells or Seal Brown.

Eye, spot on dog, tip of tail, and several border blocks

1 ounce of off-white wool.

Dog outline, corner blocks, border stripes, and strips in hit-and-miss background

4 ounces of tan wool.

"Spot" name and corner blocks

3 ounces of dusty rose wool or white wool dyed with Old Rose.

Eye pupil

Tiny speck of black.

Background

12 ounces of white wool dyed bone, 8 ounces for the background and 4 ounces for the border stripes.
Use light black walnut dye or light beige yard goods.

Hit-and-miss strips in background

Dusty Rose. 2 ounces of white wool.
Olive Green. 2 ounces of white wool.
Bronze Green. 2 ounces of white wool.
Seal Brown. 1 ounce of white wool.
2 ounces total of light brown, taupe, tan, oatmeal beige, checks, plaids, and tweeds.
Odds and ends of other compatible pinks, greens, or neutrals. I also throw in some pale "mistake" colors of an undistinguishable hue.

Border

2 ounces of gray flannel overdyed with Dark Brown or black walnut dye.
2 ounces of white wool dyed with Dark Brown.
2 ounces of white wool dyed with Seal Brown.
2 ounces of brown-and-tan herringbone or 2 ounces of neutral plaids, checks, or tweeds overdyed with Seal Brown.
2 ounces of brown plaids, neutral checks, or tweeds overdyed with Seal Brown.

DYES
(W. Cushing & Co.)

Seal Brown (or natural black walnut dye)

Old Rose

Dark Brown

Bronze Green

Olive Green

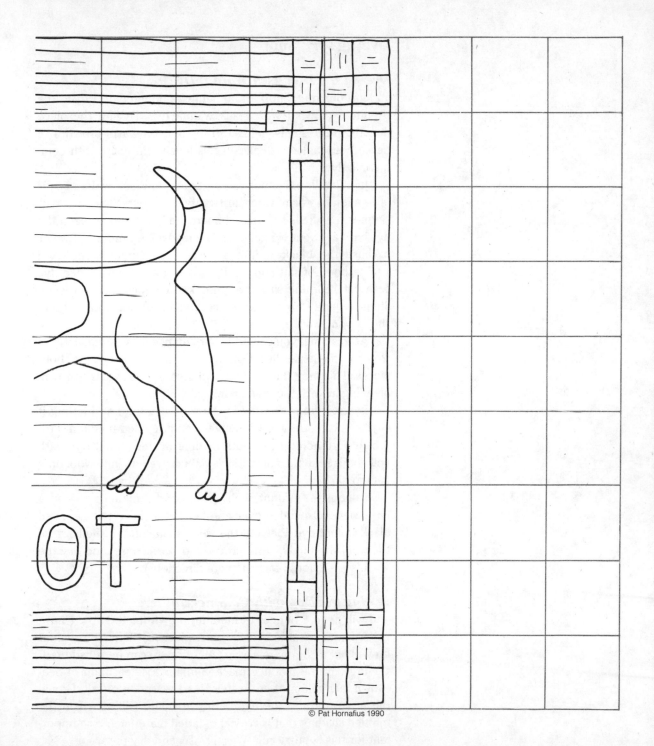

Dyeing for "Spot"

Dyeing the Dog with Walnut Dye

To lend our dog, Spot, an authentic antique color, I dyed the 6 ounces of wool with black walnut dye. Dyeing the piece directly in the shells yields a strong but soft warm brown. I've never been able to duplicate this lovely old color with commercial dyes.

In a 2-gallon dye pot, soak 2 quarts of black walnut shells in 1 gallon of warm water for twenty-four hours. The next day, simmer the shells for several hours, adding water to keep the dye bath at about 1½ gallons. You need a fair amount of water because the black walnut shells are so cumbersome. Add 1 tablespoon of salt and ¼ cup of vinegar to the leached dye bath before immersing the presoaked 6-ounce piece of wool. Simmer gently for half an hour. A vigorous boil will mat and shrink your wool.

At this time, you can add your 2-ounce gray flannel strip of wool for the border line. Continue to simmer one hour for both pieces. This gray flannel wool will dye to a very dark brown, blending in with the dog color.

By crowding the wool in the shell dye bath and letting it cool in the broth, you will achieve a variegated medium dark brown. Extending the length of time in the walnut dye bath will not deepen the color. Black walnut dye on white wool only gets so dark.

I dump the walnut shells, wool, and remaining dye in a large sieve suspended over another kettle. Save this depleted black walnut dye. Pick out the wool, shake off the shells, rinse the wool thoroughly, and proceed to wash, rinse, and dry the wool (see section II for complete directions).

Dyeing the Dog with Commercial Dyes

You will need 6 ounces of medium brown for the dog. I have never found an antique color more pleasing than black walnut brown, but a commercial dye (Seal Brown) can be substituted.

Presoak the 6-ounce piece. Simmer $6/32$ teaspoon of Seal Brown in 1 gallon of hot water plus 1 teaspoon of salt. Crowd the wet wool into the dye bath. Crowding will give you the mottled shading that is typical of faded material and so important for this country rug. Wash, rinse, and dry the wool.

If you wish to dye scraps for the hit-and-miss background or another lighter shade of brown for corner blocks, presoak your wool and add 1/32 teaspoon of Seal Brown plus 1 teaspoon of salt to a 1-quart dye bath for every 2 ounces of dry wool. This recipe will produce a lovely soft brown to mix in the background and corner blocks in the border. Wash, rinse, and dry the wool.

Dyeing the Background with Walnut Dye

The lines and small checks in the border pick up the background colors, adding darker brown for contrast. A dark border holds the rug on the ground visually. I have used up some old dull browns on hand to stripe the border bands, ranging from dark to light brown in five shades for five rows in both the inner border and the outer border. If you do not have shades of brown on hand, you can either dye with black walnut dye or use commercial dyes. I will be giving you directions for both.

Dyeing the bone background and border stripes. Save the remaining, slightly lighter black walnut dye to dye the bone shades needed for the background and border stripes. Dilute this dye in a 2-gallon kettle of water. Add 2 tablespoons of salt and ¼ cup of white vinegar to the dye bath before immersing 8 ounces of white wool for the background and 4 ounces for the border. Remove the wool when you get the bone shade you want. Wash, rinse, and dry the wool. Walnut dye can be diluted and used again and again for even lighter tints of bone. Save this lightest dye for dulling and tinting the three or four strips of wool (2 ounces each) for the rose and greens you need for the rest of the background.

Natural dyeing is experimental. Keep watching and lifting the wool so it does not become too dark for your background. Remember that natural dyes will wash and dry much lighter than commercial dyes, so dye a little deeper than the color you want.

Overdyeing for the background and corners. Your colors for "Spot" should all be dull and old looking. In other words, "dirty." If you are starting with yard goods, you'll need to dim the rose and pale green shades for the background and corner blocks with some of the light black walnut dye. This dye effectively ages the colors to blend in with the brown shades of the dog, background, and border. New colors jump out in the rug and lend a disconcerting look to an otherwise antique appearance.

Dyeing the Background with Commercial Dyes

Achieving the dusty rose. To dye the dusty rose (Old Rose) for the background and rose corner blocks, you will need a 3-ounce strip of white wool (Spot's name and corner blocks) and a 2-ounce strip of white or bone wool (background strips).

Use $\frac{1}{64}$ teaspoon of Old Rose to 1 quart of water plus 1 teaspoon of salt. This will be enough dye for a 3-ounce presoaked strip of white or a mix of half white and half bone strips. Simmer the dye bath and crowd the wool in the pan; mottling is preferable here. If you are using only white wool, lift it with a fork several times to be sure the wool receives the dye on all surfaces. If you are using bone wool, the wool can just be dumped into the pan, and not stirred or lifted, for greater variety of mottling. Wash, rinse, and dry the wool.

Use a 1-ounce strip of bone wool and a 1-ounce strip of white wool in the Old Rose dye bath for the hit-and-miss background strips. This combination will give you a clean shade and a dirty shade to mix when hooking in the background. For 2 ounces of wool, dissolve $\frac{1}{64}$ teaspoon of Old Rose plus $\frac{1}{2}$ teaspoon of salt in 1 quart of water. Immerse the presoaked wool and simmer for half an hour. Wash, rinse, and dry the wool. The more variety the better for hit-and-miss backgrounds. Hit-and-miss began as a rug-hooking technique to use up scraps of fabric. Today we can hardly find scraps, so we must create our own.

Tinting the tans. I'm assuming you can find 4 ounces of tan for the background hit-and-miss strips, the border, and the dog outline. You'll also need 2 ounces of an oatmeal beige, although pale beige plaids, checks, or tweeds can be substituted for these strips. The tan shades are used for the inner border lines and corner blocks. It is not necessary to match all of the tans. Small scraps of various shades of tan or beige work out very effectively in the corners and background strips. If you want to tint them with a few grains of Seal Brown and/or Dark Brown, they will tone into the total color scheme. Use a 1-quart pan of water plus $\frac{1}{2}$ teaspoon of salt and 1 teaspoon of white vinegar for the tinting dye bath. Wash, rinse, and dry the wool.

Achieving the bronze green. Use $1/128$ teaspoon of Bronze Green ($\frac{1}{4}$ of $1/32$ TOD teaspoon) to 3 ounces of bone or white wool or both. Use a 1-quart pan of simmering water plus 1 teaspoon of salt. Dissolve the dye and immerse the pre-soaked wool, crowding it in the pan. If you are using white wool, lift it to completely expose all the white wool to the dye bath. You do not want white spots here, but bone spots will only improve your old look, so do not stir or lift that color. Cover and simmer half an hour before washing, rinsing, and drying your wool.

Remember that $1/128$ teaspoon of Bronze Green will not dye more than 3 ounces of wool, so if you plan to add some beige, tan, or textured wool scraps, add a few more grains of Bronze Green to the pan. Use the tip of a knife for adding grains of dye. It makes them much easier to handle.

Achieving the olive green. For 2 ounces of wool, add $1/64$ teaspoon of Olive Green plus 1 teaspoon of salt to a crowded dye bath of 1 quart of water. Wash, rinse, and dry the wool.

If you need a darker tone here and there for deeper stripes in the hit-and-miss background, overdye some tan or neutral textured wool with $1/64$ teaspoon of Olive Green (about 2 ounces will do it). You cannot have too many shades of color for this rug.

Tinting the rose and greens. Save some of the lightest plaids, tweeds, or checks from the background scraps and tint with Old Rose, Bronze Green, or Olive Green to further expand your hit-and-miss palette for the background strips. The more variety, the better. Use a few grains in 1 quart of simmering water plus $\frac{1}{2}$ teaspoon of salt and 1 tablespoon of white vinegar for each of these tinting dye baths. Wash, rinse, and dry the wool. Use very little of each type of wool.

Dyeing the Border with Commercial Dyes

In all cases, simmer your dye in 1 quart of water plus 1 teaspoon of salt before immersing the 2-ounce strips of presoaked wool. Simmer each batch gently for half an hour.

Row 1. 2 ounces of gray flannel overdyed with $2/32$ teaspoon of Dark Brown dye or dyed with black walnut dye.

Row 2. 2 ounces of white wool dyed with $2/32$ teaspoon of Dark Brown dye.

Row 3. 2 ounces of white wool dyed with $2/32$ teaspoon of Seal Brown dye.

Row 4. 2 ounces of brown-and-tan herringbone tweed, or overdye a light neutral plaid, check, or tweed with $1/32$ teaspoon of Seal Brown.

Row 5. 2 ounces of brown plaid or light neutral check or tweed to overdye with $1/32$ teaspoon of Dark Brown.

Wash, rinse, and dry all the wool. This dyeing process will give you a range of five old brown shades from light to dark to use in the inner and outer border bands.

If You Don't Wish to Dye

You can have a little fun playing around with dyeing for "Spot." You can't go wrong on color as long as you stick to the dyes listed and don't start with kelly green wool or any other garish color. If you do not care to dye for this rug, however, use an old shade of brown for the dog. You may have to simmer the brown wool in warm water—lots of it—with one tablespoon of detergent for a time to remove some of the dye. Keep changing the water to remove the leached dye, but don't add any more detergent. Check this wool! Sometimes manufacturers overdye mistakes with dark colors to make them salable. I found green under a brown I had treated in this way.

Blending brown wools for the dog is also a possibility. Several shades of brown wool from remnants or used clothing can be mixed for the dog color.

Hooking "Spot"

Before beginning to hook your rug, see "Cutting the Wool" in section II.

When hooking this rug, I emulate an old rug by working in horizontal lines of hit-and-miss as it would have been hooked on a sawbuck-type frame. This means making perfectly horizontal lines in the dog and the background. Draw them in with a ruler or measuring angle. If you are positive your rug is square on the burlap, you can just follow the mesh holes, but I need directional lines here and there to ascertain horizontality. The Puritan frame I use does not enable me to see the entire field at once, and different weights of wool scraps can also throw the lines off.

Hooking the Dog

Start Spot with two loops of black for the pupil and a small row of white for the eyeball. Animals in antique rugs had small eyes, so don't let your dog's eye get too big.

Hook in a black nose, a white spot, and the tip of the tail. These areas do not have to be hooked horizontally; follow the contour of the shapes.

Now outline the dog with one row of tan. Indent for the mouth and toes. Outline the ear. Begin hooking horizontal lines at the top of the head. You will have to reverse your rows to avoid cutting off at each edge. Continue hooking the head, body, and legs.

Now you will appreciate the ability of your frame to move from side to side as you turn your rows. I watched an eighty-year-old rugmaker speed along horizontally in her sawbuck frame, going back and forth with computer-printer proficiency. Amazing! She hooked perfectly in both forward and reverse, something I cannot do. Turning my frame enables me to change the angle of my work, not my arm, thereby making horizontal hooking easier.

Finish hooking the dog with medium brown. If you are varying the choice of fabrics instead of mottling the dye, place some lighter strips here and there in the dog body to simulate fading. Don't make Spot one solid color.

Hooking the Background

After finishing the dog, hook in the corner blocks and the innermost row of dark brown to outline the border. You will then have a place to start and turn your horizontal hit-and-miss background. It is not necessary to complete all the checks in the border at this time; just make the two at each corner to complete the edge touching the background. This will keep your background corners perfectly square.

Add your initials, the date, or both in the corners before beginning the background.

Hit-and-miss backgrounds should look casual even if you spent hours dyeing and planning your colors. I place my cut bone strips (half the background) in a separate bag and cut and divide the other colors in separate bags. These strips can be 60 inches, 30 inches, 20 inches, or 10 inches in length. Different lengths of color lend interest to the field.

Begin hooking with a line of bone against the innermost dark-brown border edge. Where the strip runs out, begin another color in the same hole. Alternate the bone strips with each of the soft shades for the background as you hook. Add a darker strip (dog brown or Bronze Green) every so often for variety. You will be using twice the amount of bone to the other colors. Use two consecutive strips of bone (or a 60-inch strip) every once in a while to break up the regularity of the color placement. Be casual. This is not life or death. Use your eye to determine where to cut off your strips for color diversion.

You may want to simulate tail wagging. If so, go around the tip of the tail when hooking the background before returning to horizontal hooking. This slight rise and fall in the hit-and-miss strips will give the tail an indication of motion.

Hooking the Border

Hook in the rest of the corner blocks, alternating the direction of your hooking in a basket-weave fashion so that the blocks are square and will lie flat. Use deep rose, the dog's color, bone, dark brown, tan, dull green, or whatever wool you have the most of for your blocks. They do not have to be identical in every corner. This is a primitive rug!

You have already hooked one row of the darkest brown at the innermost edge of the field. Now finish making your five rows of various brown shades, using the dog brown for one of these rows. Keep the browns relatively close in tone, or overdye in walnut dye. You have begun with the darkest shade and will move outward with ever lighter browns.

Alternate the background bone with the tan dog outline color for the inner border band. You are hooking five rows, three bone and two tan. Begin and end with bone. Finish with five more rows on the outside border band, beginning with wool of the lightest shade of brown and ending with the darkest brown.

Finish your hooked rug by hemming it as directed in section VIII.

Wavy or Undulating Hooking

We have discussed straight-row hooking with hit-and-miss. Now let's take a look at the variations possible with wavy or undulating hooking. The backgrounds of "Little Holstein," "Little Guernsey," and "Pat's Pig" all used wavy hooking. Combined with mottled wool, wavy hooking creates a gentle movement and interest in an otherwise plain background.

Blending shades of one color in a series of undulating rows is another effective background for a simple subject if you do not care to dye. When making an antique black background, I always use this wavy technique. Combining shades of black (surprisingly enough, there are many of them), including overdyed blacks, eliminates the black-hole background created with a single value of black.

"Pat's Swan" uses the undulating hooking technique for the blues in the waves of the lake. I also used this same water technique in hooking the ocean for "Noah's Ark," framing the waves in light blue and using mottled dyeing for the water.

Courtesy of Early American Life

© Pat Hornafius 1990

"Noah's Ark" uses undulating hooking for the ocean and straight hooking for the sky. Directional hooking creates differentiated areas using the same color.

Undulating directional hooking can suggest air currents in a background simulating speed and lumpy hummocks of green in a landscape like that depicted in "American Trotter."

Most rugs are a combination of straight and curved hooking. Although early rugs made on narrow frames used typewriterlike rows, rugs designed today benefit from undulating hooking, which lends light and shadow, texture, and direction.

PATTERN

"Pat's Swan"

35 by 21 inches

MATERIALS

Swan

Body. 3 ounces of white wool.
Lines in body. ¼ ounce of off-white wool.
Beak. Scrap of gold.
Eye. Scrap of black.

Water

Waves. 1 ounce of very light blue.
Water. 4 ounces of medium mottled blue.

Hearts

4 ounces of pink wool.

Apples

3 ounces of medium red wool.

Cherries and veins in stems

1 ounce of dark red.

Stems

2 ounces of camel wool spotted with onion skins.

Leaf outline and veins

2 ounces of light yellow-green.

Leaves

2 ounces each of 4 or 5 shades of cool medium green or plaids, checks, and solids overdyed with Reseda Green.

Background

14 ounces of navy wool.

DYES

(W. Cushing & Co.)

Copenhagen Blue

Egyptian Red

Nugget Gold

Robin's Egg Blue

Reseda Green

Navy

Bright Green (optional)

Dark Green (optional)

Dyeing for "Pat's Swan"

"Pat's Swan" has a cool color scheme. The lake is shades of light blue. The border background is navy. Cherries and hearts are pink and red, which are hot colors, but they tend to the cooler, barn-red hue (Egyptian Red), not to an orangy red (Terra Cotta). For contrast, the outline of the leaves is a light yellow-green, and all the leaves lean toward shades of green on the cool side.

Dyeing the Blues

Dye the medium blue for the water with $2/32$ teaspoon of Robin's Egg Blue and $2/32$ teaspoon of Copenhagen Blue dissolved in 2 quarts of water plus 1 teaspoon of salt and ¼ cup of vinegar for rapid take-up and uneven mottling. Simmer the dye bath. Crowd the pan with the 4 ounces of white wool, but be sure all the wool surfaces touch the dye. Wait before adding the 1-ounce strip or the several strands you need for wave demarcations. The vinegar you added acts quickly, so the take-up is rapid. Robin's Egg Blue will remain in the dye bath longer than Copenhagen Blue, which absorbs first. The lighter dye that remains after a ½-minute take-up (while you are arranging the folds and exposing all the wool to the dye bath) will dye the pale blue needed for the waves. Simmer all 5 ounces of wool for thirty minutes. Remember, wet wool is darker than dry wool, so don't panic if your blues seem too dark. See section II for directions on washing, rinsing, and drying the wool.

Dyeing the Reds

Use Egyptian Red if you are dyeing the hearts, apples, and cherries. It is an old barn red that also makes a lovely light pink. Use $3/32$ teaspoon of Egyptian Red in 1 gallon of water for 3 ounces of wool for the medium red of the apples. Use $2/32$ teaspoon of Egyptian Red in 1 quart of water for the 1 ounce of dark red wool needed for the cherries. Use $1/64$ teaspoon of Egyptian Red in 1 gallon of water for the 4 ounces of wool to make the heart pink.

In all cases, dissolve the required measure of dye with 1 teaspoon of salt before immersing the presoaked white wool in each dye bath. Do not use vinegar as a mordant with Egyptian Red. It changes the color to a maroon red—not pretty! Simmer all reds for half an hour and permit the wool to cool in the dye bath for complete take-up. Wash, rinse, and dry the wool.

Dyeing the Leaf Outline

To dye the olive green shade for the leaf outline and veins, use $1/64$ teaspoon of Reseda Green and $1/32$ teaspoon of Nugget Gold plus $1/2$ teaspoon of salt in 1 quart of water for the 2 ounces of white wool. Wash, rinse, and dry the wool.

Gold for the Swan's Beak

If you need a scrap of gold for the beak, dye one strand in the Nugget Gold dye before adding the $1/64$ teaspoon of Reseda Green to the dye solution for the leaf outline. This single strand will absorb so little dye that you will not notice a color change.

Dyeing the Leaves

For the leaves, greens can be overdyed with beautiful effects. The four methods of dyeing described below will produce a variety of greens. One of them, spot dyeing, is also effective in backgrounds, grass and ground tones, animal coats, and any area of the rug that does not call for solid colors. Use your imagination and creativity to get a myriad of color effects.

Overdyeing. Done with a darker or brighter value of the same color, this is an interesting way to get a variety of leaf shades. One method is to use a number of small pieces of various tans, whites, neutral plaids, checks, and tweeds and dye them together in a green dye bath. The variety will give an overall consistency to the colors, tying them together. Dark and light green fabrics can also be added to the dye bath.

Spot dyeing. Another method is to overdye with brighter or darker colors while doing the original dye bath. Put 4 ounces of white fabric in a medium green dye bath ($1/32$ teaspoon of Reseda Green plus one teaspoon of salt in a 1-gallon dye pot) and permit the color to absorb. Then pour a solution of $1/2$ cup of water and $1/64$ teaspoon of Bright Green dye or $1/32$ teaspoon of Nugget Gold dye in puddles onto the simmering green-dyed wool. Do not stir. Permit it to absorb and then add other puddles of $1/64$ teaspoon of Copenhagen Blue or $1/64$ teaspoon of Dark Green dye solution onto the simmering wool. Since yellow and blue make green (remember your color wheel), these additions will add shadings of yellow-green and blue-green to the fabric in spots throughout the wool. Dye sparingly until the desired result is attained. When hooked, the shades will add volume and depth.

Casserole dyeing. Green wool can be spotted in a casserole or crowded in a very small pan to be overdyed. Lay wet green wool in a glass baking dish or foil-lined casserole pan. Puddle a solution of yellow or blue dye (or both) in small spots over the wool. Sprinkle it with salt to set the dye, cover with foil, and bake for thirty minutes at 250 degrees in the oven or simmer at very low heat on top of the stove. Do not let the pan boil dry. Permit the wool to cool.

Crowding wool in a pan or jar. A similar effect can be gotten by crowding wool in a very small pan with a small amount of dye on the bottom—about one inch. Scrunching the wet wool into the first dye solution on the bottom of the pan and pouring a small amount of another color on top will produce a stained-glass effect. Again, add salt to set and simmer for half an hour on very low heat. Be careful not to boil the wool dry. Add water if necessary.

If you happen to have a canning kettle and jars around the house, the wool can be put in individual jars instead of a small pan. Many jars can be steamed in the kettle at the same time, and many combinations can be achieved simultaneously.

Dyeing the Background

Dyeing the background is easy if you do not have navy blue wool. One package of Cushing dye will dye 16 ounces of wool, but I like a very dark navy for "Pat's Swan," and I use 14 ounces of wool to one package of dye. This is more fabric than is required for the rug, but you may want to add several more rows of border or keep some navy wool on hand for another project. Dissolve the dye package with 1 tablespoon of salt in a 2-gallon dye pot filled three-quarters full. Immerse the wool and simmer twenty minutes. Then add ¼ cup of white vinegar and continue simmering for ten minutes. Permit the wool to cool in the pan. Wash, rinse, and dry the wool.

Hooking "Pat's Swan"

Before hooking, see "Cutting the Wool" in section II.

Hooking the Swan

Begin with the tip of the beak and hook to the head and back again to the middle of the beak. It is always wise to begin at a point because the first pull, being a cut end, is only half of a loop and will appear smaller in the finished work. Hook in the black eye with three loops.

Outline the entire swan with white before making off-white lines in the tail feathers and several in the body. Fill in the swan by hooking in the direction of the shape to give contour to the body and tail feathers.

Hooking the Water

Outline the lake with water-blue wool. After hooking in the lighter wave lines, follow those curves and fill in the lake with medium blue, being sure to turn at the edge so the cut ends are lost somewhere in the lake.

Hooking the Border

Don't forget to add your initials and the date in a corner before completing the rest of the border.

Using the dark cherry red, hook in short lines of dark red inside the stems. Hook the stems with camel wool. Outline first, then hook in the apples. Use the same medium red to outline the dark cherries. Fill in the cherries with dark red wool. Outline and hook the pink hearts.

Outline the leaves with light yellow-green, connecting the leaf stems to the camel stems when hooking the center vein. To make the short veins that bisect the leaf, cross over the center vein and hook each leaf from side to side. Yes, you heard me! I previously stated that jumping over a finished row creates a lump and should be avoided. But skipping over one row is better than losing those tiny little veins because they are so short. Just give an extra tug to the strip when skipping over the center vein so there is not a loose bulge on the back of the rug that could pull out later. Sometimes tight bulges are better than possible future holes. Fill in the leaves with your variety of green shades.

Finish the border by outlining all of it with navy wool and filling in the rest of the navy border background. End with two straight rows of navy at the outer edges. Hem your finished rug using the directions in section VIII.

PATTERN ———————————————————————————

"Boston Baked Beans"

2 by 3 feet

MATERIALS

Pig
> 4 ounces of light pink wool.
> 1 ounce of dark pink wool.

Pig's eye, mouth, nostril, and hooves; the wheels and window outline; and the XXX on the sugar bag
> 2 ounces of black wool.

Pig harness
> Several strips of the same dark green wool as the border.

Cart
> 2 ounces of light baked-bean rust wool.

Sign and bean pot
> 2 ounces of dark baked-bean rust wool.

Factory
> 4 ounces of gray tweed, black-and-white plaid or black-and-white checks dyed maroon.

Chimney
> ½ ounce of the factory wool or a small scrap of maroon wool.

Windows and steam
> 1½ ounces of white wool.

Roof
> 4 ounces of dark gray wool or dark brown tweed.

Sky
> 6 ounces of mottled light blue wool.

Letters, wheel hub, and border
> 4 ounces of gold wool.

Sugar bags
> ⅓ ounce each of three shades of bone or light beige wool.

Grass
> 2 ounces each of four bands of olive green wool.
> 2 ounces of light and dark Reseda Green wool.

Road
> 2 ounces of gray, taupe, or light brown plaid.

Border of lamb's tongue hoops
> 6 ounces of Dark Green wool.

Background and 2 rows for the outside edge
> 8 ounces of dark brown wool.

DYES
(W. Cushing & Co.)

Terra Cotta

Mummy Brown

Robin's Egg Blue

Dark Green

Reseda Green

Egyptian Red

Copenhagen Blue

Old Gold

Nugget Gold (All Fiber Dye)

Dark Brown

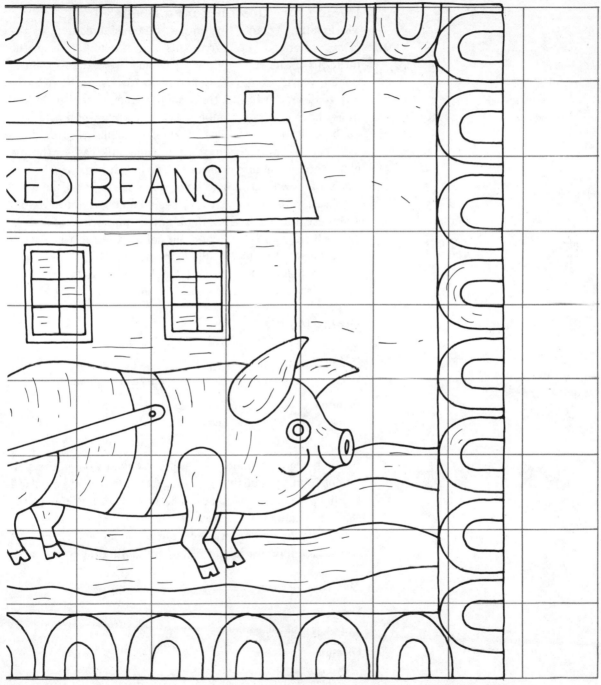

KED BEANS

Dyeing for "Boston Baked Beans"

The first time I made "Boston Baked Beans," I did not dye any of my materials. I used remnants and old clothing from the thrift shop. The roof, road, and factory were tweed jackets, ripped, washed, and cut. Baked bean rusts were from skirts. The road area was also thrift shop rejects in gray plaid and three shades of green remnants. Even the pig was a pale pink double-knit wool dress. The darker pig accents (ears and legs) were tinted with tea, which gave a tan-pink cast to the pig pink. This tea tint also dyed one of the sugar bags. The border colors of brown, green, and gold were easy to find.

"Boston Baked Beans" may seem complicated to dye, but if you use a limited color palette and combine several dyes in different ways to create your rug colors, the rug will have a warm tonality that blends all colors pleasantly.

Here follows the mix-and-match dye formulas that will assure a successful overall color scheme.

Dyeing the Pig

Pig

Body. 4 ounces of white wool.
Legs, ears, snout, and cheek line. 1 ounce of white wool.

Formula

$1/64$ teaspoon Egyptian Red, ½ teaspoon of salt, and 1 gallon of water.

Immerse the 1-ounce piece of presoaked wool in the simmering Egyptian Red dye bath first. Count to five and then add the presoaked 4-ounce piece. The first small piece, which is simmered along with the rest of the pig wool for half an hour, will be slightly darker for the legs, ears, snout, and cheek line. See section II on washing, rinsing, and drying the wool.

Dyeing the Cart

Cart

2 ounces of white wool.

Formula

$1/32$ teaspoon of Mummy Brown
$1/32$ teaspoon of Egyptian Red
½ teaspoon of salt in 1 gallon of water

This dye formula produces light Campbell baked-bean rust. If you want dark Heinz baked-bean rust, add a few grains more of Mummy Brown. Add your presoaked wool to the simmering dye solution and simmer for half an hour. Wash, rinse, and dry the wool.

Dyeing the Sign and Bean Pot

You need 2 ounces of wool. Double the cart dye formula for a rust twice as dark. Then follow the same dyeing procedure.

Formula

2/32 teaspoon of Mummy Brown
2/32 teaspoon of Egyptian Red
1 teaspoon of salt in 1 gallon of water

Dyeing the Factory

Factory

4 ounces of gray tweed or black-and-white plaid or checks. You can combine all three types of fabric if you are using scraps.

Formula

3/32 teaspoon of Terra Cotta
3/32 teaspoon of Egyptian Red
1 teaspoon of salt in 1 gallon of water

Starting out with a gray tweed or a black-and-white plaid or check will give you the depth of color you need and a texture resembling bricks. A mixture is ideal for a varied brick appearance. Overdye the material with the above formula for half an hour. Add 1 tablespoon of vinegar after fifteen minutes. Allow the overdyed wool to cool in the dye pot for complete take-up. Wash, rinse, and dry the wool.

Dyeing the Sky

I use a warm blue (if there is such a thing) for the sky in this rug.

Formula

1/32 teaspoon of Copenhagen Blue
1/32 teaspoon of Robin's Egg Blue
a few grains of Mummy Brown
¼ cup of white vinegar
1 teaspoon of salt in 1 gallon of water

Dissolve $1/32$ teaspoon of Copenhagen Blue, $1/32$ teaspoon of Robin's Egg Blue, and a few grains of Mummy Brown to dull the blue to an antique color in 1 gallon of water with the white vinegar and salt. This dye bath produces a soft French blue for the sky.

Scrunch the presoaked wool in the simmering dye bath and lift it to expose all the wool to the dye. The take-up will be rapid, so work quickly. Simmer for half an hour. Wash, rinse, and dry the wool.

Dyeing the Gold

Formula
$3/32$ teaspoon of Nugget Gold
$2/32$ teaspoon of Old Gold
1 teaspoon of salt in 1 gallon of water

I like to mix half Nugget Gold and half Old Gold for a bright but old-looking gold. Because you want a rich gold that will stand out in the small areas (letters, wheel hub, and border), use $3/32$ teaspoon of Nugget Gold and $2/32$ teaspoon of Old Gold for your 4 ounces of wool.

Dissolve the dye and 1 teaspoon of salt in 1 gallon of simmering water before immersing the presoaked wool. Do not use a vinegar mordant with yellows—it changes the color. Simmer for half an hour. Permit the wool to cool in the dye bath before washing the dyed wool, as Nugget Gold does not take up completely.

Dyeing the Sugar Bags

If you don't have three shades of beige for the sugar bags, you can tint each bag a different shade of beige using coffee or tea. For this tiny amount (⅓ ounce of white wool), use coffee for two bags and tea for one. A light bath is all that is required to stain the wool. Make a strong cup of tea, add ¼ teaspoon of salt, and simmer. Immerse the wool. The process will not take long. Check for color. Remove and rinse for a light tint. Repeat the same directions for staining with coffee. You will have to experiment: Exact proportions and simmering times cannot be given.

Dyeing the Grass

Bands of grass

2 ounces of 4 colors of varying green shades

Formula

$1/32$ teaspoon of Reseda Green
$2/32$ teaspoon of Nugget Gold
1 teaspoon of salt in 2 quarts of water

The bands of grass in the foreground are three shades of Reseda Green. For olive green, combine $1/32$ teaspoon of Reseda Green and $2/32$ teaspoon of Nugget Gold with 1 teaspoon of salt in 2 quarts of water. The two shades of olive green in the grass can be dyed at the same time by immersing the 2-ounce strip first (dark), counting to ten, and then immersing the second 2-ounce strip (medium). You can use a variety of plain white wool, pale green wool, or neutral plaids and checks to simulate grass and lend a texture to the foreground of the rug. Spot dye with the dark green formula of the lamb's tongue hoops border if you need more depth. Wash, rinse, and dry the wool.

Dye the rear bands of grass in $1/32$ teaspoon of Reseda Green.

Formula

$1/32$ teaspoon of Reseda Green
$1/2$ teaspoon of salt in 2 quarts of water

Dye the two far bands of grass at the horizon in two shades of Reseda Green. Repeating the procedure used for the grass in the foreground, immerse a presoaked 2-ounce strip first, count to fifteen, and drop in the last 2-ounce strip. You may mix in some of the Reseda strips in the foreground area to tie together the various greens of the grass.

Dyeing the Border

Lamb's tongue hoops and the pig harness

6 ounces of wool.

Formula

$1/32$ teaspoon of Old Gold
$1/32$ teaspoon of Nugget Gold
$1/4$ teaspoon of Dark Green
1 teaspoon of salt in 1 gallon of water

Combine $1/32$ teaspoon of Old Gold, $1/32$ teaspoon of Nugget Gold, and ¼ teaspoon of Dark Green for the lamb's tongue hoops with 1 teaspoon of salt and 1 gallon of water. Immerse the presoaked wool and simmer thirty minutes. After fifteen minutes, add ¼ cup of white vinegar for complete take-up. Wash, rinse, and dry the wool.

You may want to drip a little of this hot dye solution on the olive green wool discussed in the previous section. The loss of 2 tablespoons of dye will not affect the border green at all.

The brown wool border background was purchased material. If you are dyeing the dark brown wool for the border background, use 8 ounces of white wool or gray flannel to ½ teaspoon of Dark Brown dye. This is a strong dye solution, so use 1 tablespoon of salt in 2 gallons of simmering water. Add the presoaked 8-ounce piece of wool and simmer fifteen minutes before adding ¼ cup of white vinegar for complete take-up. Simmer fifteen minutes more and permit the wool to remain in the dye bath to cool. Wash, rinse, and dry the wool.

Hooking "Boston Baked Beans"

Before hooking, read "Cutting the Wool" in section II.

Hooking the Pig

Begin by making the pig details in the face. Use the darker pink for the ears, cheek line, and snout. Use black for the eye (with a white outline), mouth, nostril, and hooves.

Outline the pink pig and hook in the dark green harness. Hook the pig in a curved fashion, following the harness contours to simulate ribs. You will have to change direction for the face and legs by following the contour of each part. Complete the pig by hooking his legs and tail.

Hooking the Cart

Hook the wheels with one row of black. Hook closely, as turning a circle is difficult. Begin the cart with two rows of gold at the top, and, hooking horizontally, complete the cart with your rust wool. Hook back and forth in the wheel openings. If your wool is mottled (and I hope it is), the horizontal lines will resemble boards.

The bean pot and sugar bags are next. Hook the details first: initials, beans, steam, and the XXX on the sugar bag.

Hooking the Factory

Outline the windows in black and fill in with white wool. Outline the factory, then hook horizontally to the bottom to simulate rows of bricks. If you have dyed several shades of checks or plaids and some solid wool, drift these shades into the body of the work to break the monotony of a single color.

On the roof, hook in a single row the words "Boston Baked Beans" with gold wool. Hook closely (skip one mesh only) for a sharper image, then fill in the back of the sign with dark rust wool, outlining it first. Outline the tweed roof and hook it in horizontal rows. Complete the roof by hooking in the chimney. I save the darkest brick wool for this tiny space or use a scrap of maroon material.

Hooking the Grass and Road

Begin with the dark olive mixed foreground. Put in your initials and date with the lightest Reseda Green–dyed wool before hooking this darkest area.

I use light gray plaids, taupe-colored browns, or tweeds for the gravel road. You can mix several types of wool for the band to improve the bumpy look.

Use the lightest Reseda Green–dyed wool for the midground. I know it makes more sense to use the lightest value at the horizon, but that shade would disappear into the sky blue, so be primitive and use your contrasts where you need them.

The darkest Reseda Green–dyed wool will complete the grass area at the horizon.

Hooking the Sky

If you have not done so already, dash in undulating lines for the sky with a permanent marker. Outline the entire sky area, and hook in your mottled blue wool in this wavy fashion.

Hooking the Border

Your inner rug is now complete. Begin the border with two rows of dark brown around the outside edges. The rows will give you a place to stop and start the gold centers for the lamb's tongue border hoops, which you will hook next. Hook the dark green outer hoops, and fill in the remaining background with dark brown. See section VIII for directions on finishing your rug.

V   Motifs and Border Designs

Symmetry is an easy way to fill space, and most country rug designers used the folk art convention of mirror images. If one animal was good, two were better. In my research of antique rugs, I have uncovered an enormous number of dual-image rug designs. Always facing one another, these animals were often separated by an incongruous plant or urn of flowers in the center.

Facing birds, facing dogs, double cats, and two roosters all expanded the rug design to fill the rectangular feed bag space of approximately two by three feet. Doubling familiar images made drawing easier for unskilled artists.

Primitive rugs also used the folk art convention of a flat

A portrait of an English setter pet features a favorite Frost border pattern of garden trellis, flowers, and leaves.

© Pat Hornafius 1990

A pet rug is always a success. Take a photograph of your pet or find the breed in a dog book. This image can be blown up to the desired size if drawing the image freehand intimidates you.

plane. By that I mean they had little depth in space with no perspective. Animals and objects floated in a background without being rooted in a foundation of any kind.

Note that primitive animals were hooked in a flat manner as well. No attempt was made at naturalistic shading. Parts were identified with flat areas of color and little regard for realism.

Sources of Motifs

Ladies' magazines depicting current fashions in decor influenced country rugmakers. Aubusson rug designs with intricate flower centers and scroll borders were the first designs copied by C. S. Frost in 1868, creating a market for stamped patterns.

The Oriental craze of the last quarter of the nineteenth century was translated into rural hooked rugs with quadripartite designs cut from newspapers. Folding the paper in quarters and cutting vague Oriental shapes, rugmakers created symmetrical but unusual cutouts for rug centers. Combined with the popular fan motif in the corners, these country versions of Oriental rugs bowed to fashion trends.

Decorative accents and borders reflected ethnic motifs. Hearts, flowers, and birds were favorites of Pennsylvania Germans. New England borders featured trailing vines and flowers and scrolls with intricate turnings. With the ready accessibility

of stamped commercial patterns, most regional design differences faded, but ethnic preferences remained.

Designing Your Own Primitive Rug

Primitive rugs are not difficult to design. You can get the idea for your design from a pet, a child's drawing, or a photograph of your house. Another source is a favorite object or hobby, such as an antique car, an electric train, a boat, or a birdhouse. Anything you know and love can elicit a rug design. You will draw it well because it means something to you. You know its colors and contours. Commercial patterns fail when they depict an exotic object not in tune with the rugmaker's lifestyle and interests.

Sportsmen would appreciate a trophy fish, a deer, or a hunting dog worked into a rug design. Do your own drawing. Commercial designs of these sporting motifs become too involved and sentimental.

Your house is a wonderful subject to hook. Primitive rugs simplify, so take a photo of the front view or slightly to the side to eliminate perspective. The border could include pets, flowers from the garden, herbs if you grow them, or a collection—teacups, dolls, clocks. Make each part of your rug reflect your home and interests.

Every mother (and grandmother) has saved her child's first drawings. These are lovely mementos to hook for a child's room or to make into a larger rug combining the drawings of the whole family. I have seen a stair runner devoting one riser to each member of the family. In the runner illustrated here, the risers depict animals, house, flowers, and other vignettes meaningful to the rugmaker, and the treads are leaf forms.

Treads for the rug you design, if you are hooking a stair runner, are usually repeats. You could use leaf forms; such geometric forms as hit-and-miss and log cabin squares; intricately designed rectangles; or flower forms.

A Nantucket runner featured shells, always an interesting subject, on the risers and cat's paw (resembling jellyfish blobs) on the treads. This seaside motif was washed in shades of sandy beige, brown, pinks, and blues. Rope cables could be used at both edges of this type of seaside runner, running the length of the stair carpet. Use a stencil for the cable to keep it even and simplify your tracing.

Moses Eaton stencils are available in several books from Dover Publications, Inc. This early stenciler of both walls and furniture created a wealth of designs that can be utilized as rug-hooking patterns. Janet Warings's *Early American Stencils on Walls and Furniture* is another wonderful source of early American designs that can be translated into rug patterns and borders.

Affecting a Folk Art Style

Many of my clients have old houses filled with antiques. The rugs I make for them must blend into the surroundings in color and style. Using antique design characteristics helps to achieve the desired look.

When designing folk art animals, make the eyes smaller than today's style of large button eyes. Also, make smaller noses and mouths.

Keep the colors of your rug very muted. Dirt and fading reduced once-bright colors to soft mellow tones. Age your wools when dyeing them to match your room colors. A grain or two of the complementary color or brown or khaki (never black) will "dirty" and dull. Walnut, coffee, or tea tinting does the same trick.

Keep your subject simple, without too much detail. Using a ¼-inch strip (#8 cut) will do that for you, as realism is not possible with wide strips. Many early rugs were drawn from pasteboard designs traded and passed from one rugmaker to another. This constant use blurred the edges, softening the image. Antique hand-drawn rugs often display the almost abstract shape of a once-distinguishable object. Do not doubt your drawing ability; you can do as well. A child's drawing of a pet or house will be in the same mode.

Backgrounds can be anything from hit-and-miss stripes to mottled dyed wool. Using a variety of closely related shades of a color is also a good way to vary a background for an antique look. The ragbag provided limited amounts of a single color, so background color shifts give not only interest to the rug but also a look of authenticity.

Make an intricate border using all the leftover wools from your rug for blocks, hit-and-miss, or zigzags. Quilt patterns used as borders or cut paper designs of your own choosing are other antique border choices.

Courtesy of Mr. and Mrs. Keith Murphy

PATTERN ————————————————————————

© Pat Hornafius 1990

"Renfrew Cats"
29 by 23 inches

MATERIALS

Border blocks

Approximately 15 ounces of various colors or ½ ounce of each scrap.

Cats

6 ounces of black and charcoal black wool.
5 ounces of white wool.

Background

6 ounces of light Williamsburg blue wool.
2 ounces of medium Williamsburg blue wool.

Thin (#6 cut) red line

3 ounces of Egyptian Red wool.

Outside border rows

2 ounces of soft tan wool or background blue wool.

DYES
(W. Cushing & Co.)

Copenhagen Blue

Robin's Egg Blue

Khaki Drab

Egyptian Red

Silver Gray

Your own walnut dye to tint border colors if desired

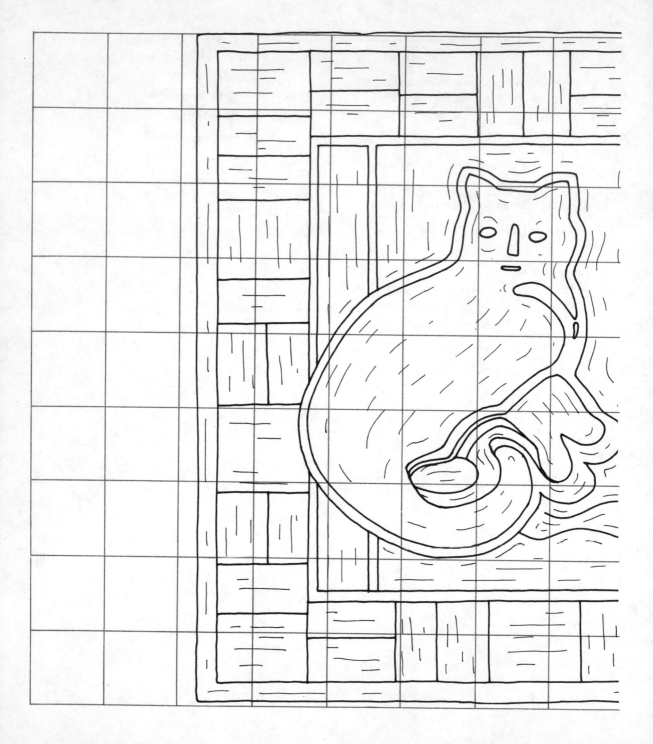

© Pat Hornafius 1990

The Design of "Renfrew Cats"

I found this antique rug in the Renfrew Museum in Waynesboro, Pennsylvania. The rug was originally dyed with natural dyes: indigo, walnut shades, old reds (madder root), and charcoal blacks. I fell in love with it immediately because of the obvious affection of the cats for each other and the old soft colors.

This rug is a perfect example of primitive rug characteristics: simple symmetrical composition, soft abstract shapes, brick path border (a quilt pattern), and flat areas of color. But what the rugmaker did with it! She personalized her cats with distinctive colors. She outlined the cats and border with a thin red line to accent the forms. She broke the border with the curve of the cats' backs and joined them at their paws to bring the composition together. The decisions were instinctive, I'm sure, and not consciously planned, but her leap of imagination makes "Renfrew Cats" an exceptional folk art design. If you plan to adapt the design to make cat portraits of your own pets, change the color scheme to adjust to calico cats, gray cats, and so on.

Dyeing for "Renfrew Cats"

This rug would look equally beautiful with a Reseda Green background rather than a blue one. Use the green formula from the "Little Holstein" pattern and overdye some of your textured wools in the same color of green for the border.

There are fifty-six blocks in the border of this rug. Four corner blocks are the same color. I used thirty colors or shades in the border, but you could do with fewer. Plan your color division so that the various lights, darks, and mediums are scattered around the border, thereby balancing the color scheme.

I made eleven blocks walnut white. Use varying shades of walnut or shades of beige. The four corner blocks are old red (Egyptian Red) to match the thin red line. Overdye plaids, checks, and tweeds with this red or the Williamsburg blue that you will be using for the background. I used scraps from the background and overdyed wools for eight blue blocks. Scatter some charcoal blacks from the cats in the border, one on each side. The remaining blocks can be soft blue tweeds, taupes, oatmeal beige, tans, and checks (overdyed with walnut tint if necessary). The beauty of this border is in its randomness and soft colors.

Dyeing the Background

The Williamsburg blue I have developed is an old, faded indigo blue. Natural indigo blue has a tinge of green, which I tried to duplicate with the addition of Khaki Drab. The formula for the six ounces needed for the background plus another two ounces for the cats' mat is as follows:

$4/32$ teaspoon of Copenhagen Blue
$2/32$ teaspoon of Robin's Egg Blue
$1/32$ teaspoon of Silver Gray
$1/64$ teaspoon of Khaki Drab

Dissolve all these dyes in a large kettle of hot water and add 1 teaspoon of salt. Presoak the wool and drop the 2 ounces for the slightly darker shade of the cats' mat into the simmering dye bath. Count to fifteen before immersing the 6-ounce background piece, and simmer for half an hour. Cool the wool in the dye bath for complete take-up. See section II for directions on washing, rinsing, and drying the wool.

If you are planning to overdye other plaids or checks in Williamsburg blue, make another solution. Adding more wool to this one will lighten the background color by using up the dye. The above basic formula will overdye 8 ounces of wool for blue blocks. Dye the wool for the blocks separately, as some of the plaids and checks may run. Halve the dye amounts if you plan to overdye only 4 ounces of wool. Use the same dyeing procedure as described above for your background material.

Dyeing the Border

A few black walnut shells soaked overnight and simmered for one day will yield enough dye to tint the several ounces of white wool needed for the border. Natural dyes have no exact amounts. Strain the liquid. Add 1 teaspoon of salt to 1 quart of plain water plus 1 tablespoon of white vinegar. Use this to dilute the walnut dye to a pale shade of brown. Test this natural dye with a small strip to judge its color. The wool will be lighter after being washed.

To tint other colors that may appear too bright for your

border, you may use this light walnut bath or one of coffee or tea. Coffee stain is a yellow brown; tea stain is a pinkish tan. Steep 1 cup of strong tea or use a very strong cup of coffee in 2 cups of water. Add salt and vinegar and test for tint color. All these natural dyes need salt and vinegar to set the stain. Immerse your wools and simmer until the correct color is attained. Wash, rinse, and dry the wool. Be sure you don't have a bleeder in some of your wools, or the whole lot may end up mud-colored. Dye the fabrics separately if you're worried.

Dyeing the Egyptian Red

You will need about 1½ to 2 ounces of red wool cut $6/32$ inches, or #6 cut, for the thin red line around the cats and border. Cut only as much as you need for this outline, and save the rest (1 ounce) for the red corner blocks, which are cut ¼ inches, or #8 cut.

To dye the 3 ounces of white wool with Egyptian Red, dissolve $3/32$ teaspoon of Egyptian Red dye, plus 1 teaspoon of salt, in a 1-quart dye pot of hot water. Simmer to dissolve the dye before immersing the presoaked wool. If you crowd the pan, you will achieve the mottled look so important for old-looking rugs. Lift the wool several times to be sure all the wool is exposed to the dye bath, eliminating white spots, then cover and simmer half an hour. Permit the wool to cool in the dye bath for complete take-up. Wash, rinse, and dry the wool.

Hooking "Renfrew Cats"

Before beginning to hook your rug, see the directions on cutting the wool in section II. You will be using #6-cut strips for a small section of this rug. The rest of the rug uses #8 strips.

Hooking the Cats

Begin by hooking in the cats' faces. Keep their features small. Outline the cats with the thin red line (#6 cut), then outline inside that row with one row of white. Some of the white cat and white sections of the black cat flow into the border, which may look confusing, but it all works out in the end. The interplay of black and white is important to this design. Hook the black and white cats, following the contour of the cats' shapes.

Mix your blacks for an antique look. If you have shades of white and off-white, mix them as well.

Hook in the cats' mat, and outline red and white between the border and field before beginning the background.

Hooking the Background

Always begin the background by hooking the inside edges and a row of background color around the cats. This technique stabilizes your shapes and squares off your background corners.

Because you have curved the direction of the rows for the cats, you may want to make straight vertical or horizontal rows in the background. The bands of background under the cats and at the outer edges will be straight rows, but hook as you like for the center and top sections.

Hooking the Border

Choose a soft tan or the background blue for two rows outside the border. These rows will keep your blocks true and your border straight.

Hook the corner blocks first. Add your initials in one corner and perhaps the date in another corner.

In plotting your various colored blocks, remember to contrast light against dark so as not to lose any of the rectangles in the overall color scheme. Be sure to include several charcoal (but not black) bricks, one on each side of your rug, to draw the black-cat color into the border. Solid black bricks would be too dark and would dominate the other blocks.

Hook the border blocks in a basket-weave fashion for textural interest and to keep the border edges flat. Hooking all the blocks in the same direction might stretch the burlap and result in a rippled edge.

If you run out of a color while hooking a brick, don't despair. Combine several shades in some of the blocks (not just one) to use up ends. Country rugmakers did not agonize over color choices. They just grabbed and used. This border is an elevated form of hit-and-miss, but do try to hit!

To finish your rug, follow the directions given in section VIII.

You may run the cable border design right off the pattern at each end of the rug or butt the cable against a corner block featuring a star, rosette, or other quilting motif.

Graduating the angled colors from darkest dark to lightest light creates a very interesting border. Use at least two rows of every color to get the light-and-shadow effect.

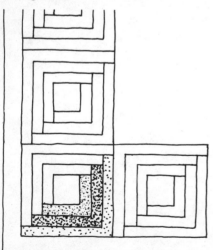

Designs for Borders

Early country rugs had simple borders, if any at all. Often the borders wore away, unraveled, and were rebound, losing the pattern. Later, during the Oriental rug craze of the late nineteenth century, multiple borders were copied to enliven country hooked rugs. Of course, the rural interpretations were far from authentic, but bands of borders left less room in the center for the rug artist to worry about, and simple quatrepartite cutouts could do the job.

When planning your rug borders, remember one maxim—simple center, fancy border; fancy center, simple border. When in doubt, err on the side of simplicity. "Less is more" in country rugs.

Quilt patterns were the traditional source of border designs in country rugs. Quilting diagrams can be used for hooking a border. On an Amish Bar hooked rug I made for a rug workshop, I used a quilting diagram for a cable border, transferring it to the burlap. Because Amish quilt borders are often black, I used several shades from charcoal to dead black, placing stars in each corner. Hooking these cables in bands of color gave a very subtle light-and-shadow effect to the border, like light striking quilted surfaces. The same treatment would be equally effective using shades of white and off-white to create a quilted border design.

Such quilt patterns as log cabin, variations on triangles, brick path, sawtooth, and checkerboards can all be adapted to rug borders.

A log cabin border is a colorful light-and-shadow design. Half the right angles are dark on one side of the block. The other half uses lighter colors in the right-angle rows. Use a warm bright color in the center block to resemble a light in the window.

Quilt books show many variations on log cabin. You could even do an entire rug in this design. It is a wonderful pattern for using up small amounts of wool.

Zigzags

Triangles, called chevrons or zigzags, were popular as border designs. Easily drawn and a good place to use leftovers, zig-

Courtesy of Early American Life

© Pat Hornafius 1990

"Mary's Lamb," a Pennsylvania German version of a Frost lamb, features a complex home-drawn triangle border.

Simple chevrons separate triangles in a border. Beware of corners! Triangles can meet or be divided by a 45-degree angle bar to finish the corner design.

zags were a hit-and-miss arrangement, as intricate as the rugmaker chose to make them.

To plan a zigzag border, determine the size of your finished rug and find the common denominator. I like rugs 24 by 36 inches because the common denominator for this size can be 3, 4, or 6 inches. Decide how many and how close you wish your triangles to be.

If you plan to use dots or dividers inside the triangles, make the triangles bigger. To use a variety of scrap materials in a series of rows inside the triangles, make the triangles big enough to accommodate the many ¼-inch strips. You can alternate plain triangles and striped chevrons in this type of border.

After you have determined the size of the triangles, fold the paper in an accordion style the length of your vertical and horizontal edges and cut your triangle shape. Opened up, this pattern should serve as your sawtooth border.

Blocks

Blocks of various styles—log cabin, bricks, basket weave, hit-and-miss, and square checks—were other simple border devices that used up leftover colors. "Little Guernsey" and "Little Holstein" use a simple block pattern border. "Renfrew Cats" uses a rectangular brick design in its border.

Border blocks can be made in hit-and-miss to enliven a

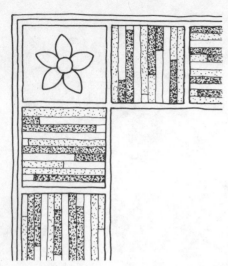

"Catch of the Day" (above right) has a simple block-and-rectangle border that provides contrast to the undulating waves in the water. To add interest to a hit-and-miss border (above), place a motif echoing the center of the rug in each corner. Hooked on a solid background-colored block, it will carry out the rug colors and anchor the corners.

static or symmetrical rug design. Hook alternate blocks in a basket-weave fashion to ensure a flat border edge. Border blocks in hit-and-miss really use up the small scraps, so don't throw away any strips over 6 inches long. Keep these small pieces in a box for eventual use. For 3-inch border blocks, with a large variety of color and pattern, I cut my strips about 8 inches long. Lengths longer than 8 inches would dominate the block. You need about four to six different colors per block.

When hooking hit-and-miss blocks, be sure to turn the strip and reverse directions before cutting off the end. Nothing looks worse (or creates a weaker rug) than a long line of cut ends at the edge of the rug or border blocks. Make your cuts in various places in the field, as you would for any background.

In "ABC Teddy Bear," a border of alphabet blocks dominates the design. I used the printing style and primary colors of children's wooden blocks.

"Harry's Pig" uses a pointed-block border design to emulate a fence with plain corner posts. For this pink pig in a mottled khaki-green sty, I variegated the pickets in shades of tan, beige, walnut, and light brown to imitate wood.

Curves

Clamshell and lamb's tongue created curved interest in borders. These overlapping cup or lid shapes were easy to trace. Country women used tracing aids that were at hand: teacups, Mason jar lids, or small plates.

"Boston Baked Beans" employs a lamb's tongue border, as does "Puppy with Targets." "Puppy with Targets" is a boy's rug. The brown puppy fearfully stealing a glance at the target bor-

A clamshell border (below) uses overlapping circles. They can be as deep as you care to make them, extending the depth of the border. "Puppy with Targets" (left) is an elaborate combination of lamb's tongue and blocks that suggest children's games.

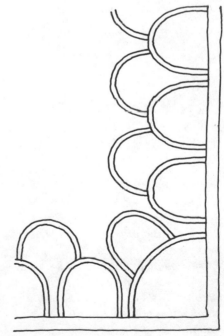

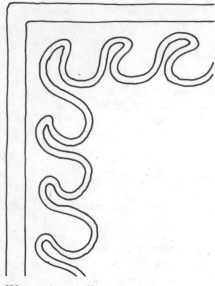

*Waves, in small crests, were
cut using folded paper. Generally
outlined in a contrasting color,
waves create an appropriate border
for a nautical rug.*

der was made for a young man who loved archery and checkers (see the corners). The colors are shades of brown (dog), red (background), off-white, beige, and black. Repeating these colors in the elaborate lamb's tongue targets and checkerboard corners creates a simple and masculine color scheme.

Undulating Curves

The undulating curve cut from folded paper was another simple border device. By the same paper-cutting method, waves, Greek key, and sawtooth designs were created for the border treatment.

To make an undulating curve to fit your finished rug border, cut a piece of paper to the same dimensions. Decide how many curves will fit on the vertical and horizontal edges. Use the common denominator for each side. A 24-by-36-inch rug will have a common denominator of 3, 4, or 6 inches. Fold your paper pattern in one of these measurements. The more folds there are, the more undulating curves will be created. Cut a simple curve, keeping an inch or two from the edge. This curve will determine the depth of the border. When opened, the undulating curves will fit the edges of the border. To turn the corner, join the curves and swing around to begin the other side. Trace the undulating curves around all the sides.

Simple undulating borders benefit from the use of various materials. The deeper the curve, the more colors can be worked in. Use bands of harmonizing fabrics to enliven such borders.

*Borders using plaid material benefit
from undulating hooking. The plaid
fabric has plenty of interest in itself.
It just needs shape and texture
(created by the curved rows) to make
an effective border. "Rooster with
Rabbit Cart" uses this technique.*

Dominant Border Designs

Sometimes the border becomes as important as the rug design itself. "Doves with Pansies" uses a curving vine of pansies and leaves to dominate the simple Love Dove design. In a similar fashion, "Pat's Swan" uses apples and cherries to frame the subject matter.

When silhouetted against the background color, such gentle vines, like the leaves and acorns of the accompanying illustration, create graceful and undemanding border motifs.

Stripes

Rows of stripes, employing the last of the rug scraps, draw the rug colors into the border. Alternating with the background color, this is a soft and undemanding border treatment.

In some rugs with striped borders, it might be appropriate to hook a corner motif against the border background to make a visual connection with the center of the rug.

To make the picot edge on the striped border illustrated here, jump out every fourth loop into the background. When hooking the background between the picot loops, merely skip over the outlying loop and continue to fill in that single row against the edge.

The semicircular border of drooping acorns was taken from the border of the earliest-known hooked rug (circa 1840).

Simple stripes alternate lights and darks, using a corner motif against the border background.

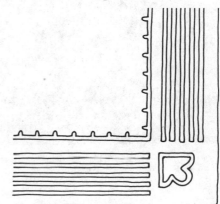

PATTERN

© Pat Hornafius 1990

"Doves with Pansies"

2 by 3 feet

M A T E R I A L S

Doves

8 ounces or ¾ yard of white wool to dye or old blue wool (this amount includes enough wool for the pansies).

Outline of doves and leaves

6 ounces of very pale walnut, very light beige, or off-white wool.

Outlines of pansies, petals, and buds

3 ounces or ¼ yard of white wool dyed very light dull pink.

Pansies

2 ounces each of four or five shades of mauve-pink, ranging in color from palest pink to rich maroon wool.

Leaves

2 ounces each of three or four shades of olive green wool.

Stems

4 ounces of tan or camel wool.

Background

20 ounces of either overdyed maroon wool or red plaids over-dyed black.

D Y E S
(W. Cushing & Co.)

Copenhagen Blue

Robin's Egg Blue

Silver Gray

Khaki Drab

Maroon

Black

Olive Green

Reseda Green

Bronze Green

Walnut dye, coffee, or tea to tint (optional)

© Pat Hornafius 1990

Dyeing for "Doves with Pansies"

"Amish Doves" is an authentic Amish rug design of the late nineteenth century. Peace Doves are favorite Amish motifs. Found in quilts as well, doves are symbols of the pacifist tenets of the Plain faith. In recent times these birds have been transposed into Love Doves and are found on wedding quilts.

Pansies, because of their brilliant colors, preferably purple, grace many Amish gardens. Their bright combinations of shades appeal to the Amish love of color.

For the antique black background of my version of this rug, I overdyed maroon wool and red plaids with Black dye. This hint of color enlivens what would otherwise be a very drab and dead background.

Because the rug design is truly antique, the color scheme we will use is dull and muted, and will give you an idea of how to antique any color scheme for an authentic old look. Rather than merely tinting each shade with walnut, tea, or coffee to dim its color, we will learn how to add complements (or opposites) to age the hues.

This technique is tricky and needs a very light touch. A few grains of each complement added to the dye bath are enough. We do not want to lose the color but merely age it. Remember the color wheel from section III and refer to it if necessary.

The indigo blue of the doves does not have to be muted, as it is a replica of a natural dye and is mellow to begin with. The pinky-mauves of the pansies present a problem if you are using commercially dyed pink or mauve material. Green yard goods may also have to be dulled, but olive green is already rather drab, so it may be all right. Use your eyes. Throw the materials on the floor beside the background color before you cut them. If any color looks too bright or bold, you may have to dim it a little.

Dyeing the Doves

For 8 ounces of white wool, dissolve the following:

$2/32$ teaspoon of Copenhagen Blue
$1/32$ teaspoon of Robin's Egg Blue
$1/32$ teaspoon of Silver Gray
$1/64$ teaspoon of Khaki Drab

Use a 2-gallon dye pot filled three-quarters full of hot water. Add 1 teaspoon of salt and simmer. Drop the presoaked wool into the dye bath and simmer for half an hour. The take-up will be slow because of the salt, so permit the wool to cool in the dye bath before washing it. See section II for directions on washing, rinsing, and drying the wool.

Dyeing the Pansies

If you have pale pink wool, you may need to dull it for this antique color scheme. Add one or two grains of Olive Green dye, depending upon the amount of pink wool used, to a 1-quart pot of simmering water. Immerse the pink wool. If this solution doesn't do the job, remove the wool, add a few more grains to the dye bath, and redip the wool. You may want to dye one strip first, rinse, and dry it to determine the correct amount of drabbing.

To darken the pink yard goods to the deeper shades needed for the pansies, tear off several 2-ounce strips. Dissolve $1/64$ teaspoon of Maroon dye plus $1/4$ teaspoon of salt in a small pot of water. Dip these strips consecutively into the Maroon tint, counting to fifteen between immersions. Simmer for half an hour. Wash, rinse, and dry the wool.

I prefer to dye my own fabric from scratch. This way I have complete control over the shades I want. For dyeing all four or five shades of pansy pink from very light (the outlines) to deepest maroon (the center petal), use Maroon dye.

Pink for the outline. Use $1/3$ of $1/32$ teaspoon (yes, I know this is a minuscule amount) of Maroon dye in 2 quarts of water plus $1/2$ teaspoon of salt. Immerse the 3-ounce strip and take it out at once. This is your lightest shade.

A slightly darker shade of pink. Immerse the second strip of white wool (2 ounces) in the dye bath. Permit it to take up completely by simmering for half an hour.

The darkest shade of pink. After removing the second strip, add $1/64$ teaspoon of Maroon dye plus 1 tablespoon of white vinegar to the boiling water. Simmer before adding the 2-ounce piece that will be your darkest strip.

The middle two shades of pink. The strip that will be the darkest shade of pink is simmering in the dye pot. Permit it to simmer for one minute before adding another 2-ounce strip.

You should get a medium dark shade of pinky-mauve from this strip. Count to 15 and add another strip for a medium pink shade. Finish the dyeing process by simmering all three strips for half an hour.

The darkest maroon. You may want a real maroon color for your initials and the date, perhaps for even darker petal spots in the pansies. If you need this darker color, use $1/32$ teaspoon of Maroon dye to 1 quart of water plus ½ teaspoon of salt and 1 tablespoon of white vinegar. Add a 1-ounce piece of black-and-white plaid or check material for this darkest area. The plaid will add a different texture and a mottled look to the flower spots, initials, and date.

Wash, rinse, and dry all the shades of pink wool.

Dyeing the Leaves
The outline of the leaves can be the same pale beige as your dove outline or a very light shade of olive green. You will be dyeing in sequence, as you did for the pansies. If you have a light neutral plaid or check, use a strip of this material for one of your greens. Dissolve the following:

$1/32$ teaspoon of Olive Green

$1/32$ teaspoon of Reseda Green

$1/32$ teaspoon of Bronze Green

1 teaspoon of salt

Use a 1-gallon pot filled three-quarters full of hot water. Simmer the dye bath and prepare your strips. You will need three 2-ounce strips of white wool and 3 more ounces of white wool if you plan to dye the lightest green shade for the outline of the leaves.

As you dyed the lightest light pink for the pansy outline, so dye the lightest light-green shade for the leaf outline. Immerse the 3-ounce strip and remove it at once. Simmer this first pale outline strip in a separate pan with 2 inches of water for thirty minutes to allow the dye to mature.

If you have a check or plaid strip, add it next for the deepest shade, then move on to the plain white wool strips. Count to ten between immersing each strip for a slight change in depth of color. You will see that the strip added first will become darker with time in the dye bath, and each subsequent strip will be a shade lighter than its predecessor. The strips can all simmer together except for the pale outline, which you removed immediately after immersing. Wash, rinse, and dry all the green wool.

Dyeing the Background

You will need about 20 ounces of maroon, red plaid, or other dark colors to overdye black. Use black material at your own risk. Solid black backgrounds are deadly. If you use my technique of overdyeing, the original warm color, although overdyed, will shine through, giving your background a warm mellow glow. The background says, "I am black," but we know it isn't so.

Use your largest kettle (at least 2 gallons) for this dye bath. You want your wool and dye to circulate in the pot for a complete dye take-up and even dye color. Use 2 tablespoons of salt when dissolving the Black dye (one package for 20 ounces).

Simmer the dye bath while presoaking the mixture of wools in warm water. Immerse the lightest and brightest pieces of wool first, then the darker colors. If you are using all maroon wool, dump it in all at once. Stir and lift the wool to be sure that all surfaces are submerged in the black dye. Simmer fifteen minutes before adding ½ cup of white vinegar. Simmer fifteen minutes more and permit the wool to cool in the dye bath. Wash, rinse, and dry the wool.

Hooking "Doves with Pansies"

Before beginning to hook your rug, see "Cutting the Wool" in section II.

Hooking the Doves

Begin hooking the doves with the pale beige, off-white, or very pale walnut-white strips. Hook the eyes, then begin the outline with the beak. I always start a sharp point with the first loop, as it is half of a loop and will appear smaller in the finished work. Outline the birds and wings, hooking each feather separation individually. Now, following the contour of the dove, fill in the body, tail, and wings with your blue wool.

Hooking the Border

First, hook in the camel or tan stems in two rows. Next, outline each section of the pansy petals and make several loops in the center of each flower. Outline the buds and extend the outline to the stem (one row) for a tiny branch.

Fill in the pansies with all the shades of pink, mauve, and blue, reserving the deep maroon for the pansies' faces or large spots. Try to change the location of these colors in the flower, making each pansy different from the rest. Varying the spots and petals eliminates the cookie-cutter sameness found in commercial rugs.

Fill in the buds half-and-half, varying each color combination. If you find yourself running low on one color, substitute another, and make do as old-time rug hookers did.

Outline the leaves in the palest green or off-white of the bird outline. Extend the outline to the stem. Fill in each leaf following the contour, beginning at the point and ending somewhere in the middle. Interchange your three or four shades of green at will.

Hooking the Background

Before beginning to hook the background, put in your initials and the date. It is important for future generations to know when grandma made this rug. I hook the date for another reason. Some of my rugs look very old, and antiques dealers enjoy passing them off as antiques. My sister found one of my rugs at an antiques mall (yes, a contradiction in terms) being sold as a nineteenth-century rug. I am not that old!

Begin the background by outlining the doves and all the flowers and vines. Hook the area between the birds in a horizontal direction, then fill in the rest of the background.

End the background with several rows on the outside edge. To finish your rug, see hemming directions in section VIII.

PATTERN ⸺⸺⸺⸺⸺⸺⸺⸺⸺⸺⸺⸺⸺⸺⸺⸺⸺⸺

© Pat Hornafius 1990

"Little Lamb Pulltoy"

26 by 17½ inches

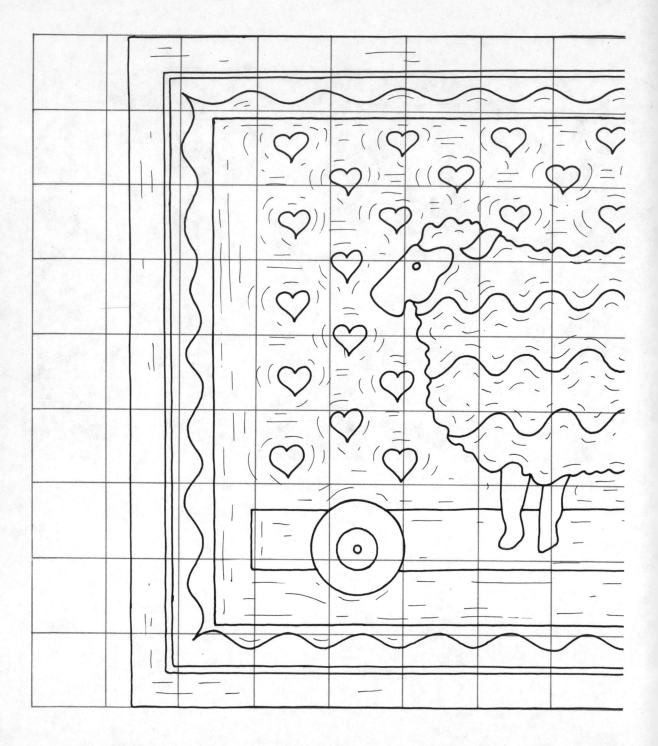

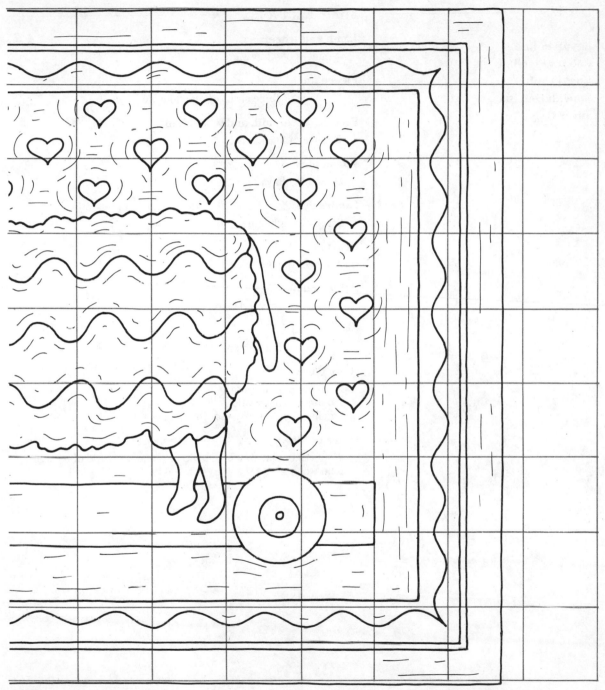

DYES ————————————————
(W. Cushing & Co.)

Egyptian Red
Robin's Egg Blue
Khaki Drab
Copenhagen Blue
Silver Gray

MATERIALS ————————————————————————

Lamb and wheels
   4 ounces of white wool.

Fleece lines
   ¼ ounce or three strips of off-white wool.

Face, legs, ear, tail, and wheel hubs
   1 ounce of black wool.

Wheel pins
   Scrap of gold wool.

Lamb's eye
   Scrap of bright blue wool.

Hearts
   2 ounces of pink wool.

Pulltoy stand
   2 ounces of rosy-red wool.

Background
   8 ounces of light blue wool.

Wavy border
   2 ounces of pink wool.
   2 ounces of navy wool.
   Small amount of rosy-red wool (pulltoy stand).

Outer border
   4 ounces of pink-and-blue plaid or a deeper shade of background
   blue wool.

"Little Lamb Pulltoy" is a charming rug for a child's room. It is shown in Williamsburg blue, but I have made it in Reseda Green (see "Little Holstein" directions for dyeing), changing only the color of the background and substituting dark green for the navy in the border.

Without the hearts in the background and the pulltoy base, "Little Lamb Pulltoy" is also effective with the lamb standing in a meadow of green grass with a pale-blue mottled sky.

If you wish to enlarge "Little Lamb Pulltoy" to approximate the size of "Little Holstein," you could design a whimsical country rug with a "sheep in the meadow, a cow in the corn" motif. Or, by reducing them, you could have a group of each grazing on opposite hills of grass and corn. I have always wanted to make this design but haven't gotten around to it yet. If you beat me to it, send me a photograph. I know it will be a success.

Dyeing for "Little Lamb Pulltoy"

Dyeing the Background
Use Williamsburg blue for the background. For 8 ounces of white wool, use the following:

$4/32$ teaspoon of Copenhagen Blue

$3/32$ teaspoon of Robin's Egg Blue

$1/64$ teaspoon of Silver Gray

$1/64$ teaspoon of Khaki Drab

1 teaspoon of salt in 1½ gallons of water

Dissolve the dyes with the 1 teaspoon of salt in a 2-gallon dye pot filled three-quarters full of water. Simmer the dye bath before immersing the presoaked wool. You want a relatively even dye for this background, as the hearts will add enough interest to the background texture. Simmer for about half an hour, checking the color and removing your wool when the depth of color is correct for your rug. I prefer a deep color, but you may want more of a pastel for a baby's room.

If the pastel hue you desire takes up before the dye matures (half an hour), transfer the wet wool to another kettle as soon as it reaches the hue you want and let it steam in its own juices for the remaining time. Robin's Egg Blue is the last color to take up, so your wool may become a bit duller than if it matures for the full half-hour in the original dye bath. See section II for directions on washing, rinsing, and drying the wool.

Dyeing the Reds
Egyptian Red will give you the two values of red color you need for this rug.

For the hearts and inner border section, you need 4 ounces of white wool. Dissolve 1/64 teaspoon of Egyptian Red in a 1-gallon pot of hot water. Add ½ teaspoon of salt. This solution will make a warm pale pink for your hearts and wavy border. Boil the dye before immersing the presoaked wool, and then allow the wool to simmer for half an hour. Wash, rinse, and dry the wool.

To dye the pulltoy stand and border line, you need 2 more ounces of white wool. Follow the above directions, using 1/64 teaspoon of Egyptian Red plus ½ teaspoon of salt in 1 quart of water, for a rosy-red for the pulltoy stand and for a single row of hooking at the border. Crowd the wool in a 1-quart pot. Mottling looks great here. Simmer for half an hour. Wash, rinse, and dry the wool.

Dyeing the Outer Border
The outside border can be a blue-and-pink plaid, or you can dye another 4 ounces of white wool or very pale plaid or checks with the same Williamsburg blue formula used for dyeing the background. Since you are dyeing half the amount of wool (4 ounces as opposed to 8), halve the amount of dye required, but add 2 tablespoons of white vinegar in the initial dye bath for a mottled look to slightly change the appearance of the border edge. Add 2 more tablespoons of vinegar after fifteen minutes of simmering, and complete the half-hour maturing time. Wash, rinse, and dry the wool.

Dyeing the Details
The tiny scrap required for the bright blue eye can be dyed with a few grains of Copenhagen Blue in a 1-quart pan with ½ teaspoon of white vinegar and 2 inches of simmering water for ten minutes.

The tiny gold scrap needed for the wheel pins can be dyed with a teaspoon of turmeric plus ½ teaspoon of salt in a small pan with 1 cup of water. Simmer for fifteen minutes, and cool the scrap in the pan. This natural dye can be found on your spice shelf. If you have Nugget Gold dye on hand, dye the strip with a few grains plus ¼ teaspoon of salt in 1 cup of boiling water for ten minutes. Wash, rinse, and dry the detail wools.

Dyeing the Lamb and Fleece

I assume you have white wool for the lamb and off-white or light beige for the wavy fleece lines. If you want to tint the three strips of wool for the fleece lines, you can use a cup of coffee or a cup of strong tea. They are natural dyes (as every dentist knows), and a short simmer of ten minutes in one of them plus ½ teaspoon of salt will produce an off-white for the three wavy lines. Wash, rinse, and dry the wool.

Use small scraps of black wool for the ear, nose, tail, legs, and wheel hubs.

Final Preparations

Before beginning to hook your rug, see the directions on cutting the wool in section II.

Cutting Wool for the Hearts

The tiny hearts in this rug require a #6 cut (6/32 inches) to complete the shape. A #8-cut strip (¼-inch) is too wide.

You must cut thirty-five thin strips of pink for your hearts with the #6 cutting blade. Tear the 4-ounce piece of pink wool in half lengthwise before cutting the hearts. Cut 2 ounces with the #6 blade for the hearts, and 2 ounces with the #8 blade for the wavy border.

Each heart takes one 15-inch length of #6-cut wool. As you slit your wool on the #6 cutter, count the usable strips. The sides may be too frayed from tearing to be usable. Continue cutting until you have thirty-five usable thin strips, each 15 inches long.

Hooking "Little Lamb Pulltoy"

Hooking the Lamb and Pulltoy Stand

Begin hooking with the tiny pieces: the eye and wheel pins. Make the three single rows of undulating lines in the lamb body to simulate fleece. Hook the black face, ear, tail, and legs.

Make the black wheel hub as well. Hook the white wheels. Outline the lamb, and then hook the lamb body, following the contours of the fleece lines. Outline and hook horizontal rows for the pulltoy stand.

Hooking the Hearts
Outline the hearts, starting at the point; then hook the centers. Finish each heart with a single strip. Hooking these tiny hearts may drive you crazy, but there are only thirty-five!

Hooking the Background
After completing the hearts, move on to the background. Outline the lamb, stand, and wheels. Hook in your initials, the date, and a row around the wavy border edge. Now the fun begins. Outline each heart several times with background blue before beginning the entire field. Starting at one side of the border edge, hook horizontally around the heart forms, following the contour of each before proceeding to the next one. Be sure to turn around at your far edge (do not cut off the strip here) and continue back, hooking above or below each heart as you come to it.

Hooking the Borders
Having proven yourself an accomplished hooker with the background, now take on undulating rows of border.

Begin with the inside pink border. Hook a straight edge against the background before beginning the undulating edge. These two rows should touch in the narrow section, leaving you to fill in the bulges with a smaller piece. Repeat the technique for the navy undulating section.

Hook one row of rosy-red before completing the outside edge of four or five rows of deep blue. To complete the hemming and binding of your finished rug, see the directions in section VIII.

Pattern and Texture

VI

Pattern and texture create surface interest. Pattern is the visual appearance of a surface. Tree branches shadowed on the lawn, flowers growing in the garden, waves in the sea, designs printed on fabrics—all create pattern with light and shadows, color, repetition, and variety.

To visualize pattern and distinguish it from color, think of a black-and-white photograph. Even without color, pattern creates a surface design.

Texture is the tactile feel of a surface: furry animals, woolly tweeds, ruffled feathers, spiky grasses, and gravel roads. We simulate texture in a basically two-dimensional art by the use of a variety of different wools.

Primitive rug hookers depend upon a wide selection of types of woven fabrics: tweeds, checks, plaids, stripes, herringbones, and the many shades of one color used in blending. Mottled dyeing to variegate a surface is still our best resource for pattern and texture.

Texture is also created by the width and height of rug loops. The #8 cut for ¼-inch strips gives a height of ¼ inch, which offers the hooked rug a lot of surface texture in the play of light and shadow on the pile.

Low thin hooked loops used in tapestry hooking create a flatter appearance. A rug having this smooth, flat pile does not have a great amount of surface texture and can therefore create surface interest with more shading and detail. Primitive rugmakers are not tapestry hooking but painting with broader and bolder strokes.

Technique in Primitive Rugs

Rug designs depicted earlier in this book show relatively plain subjects and backgrounds, relying on mottled dyeing to increase surface interest. As you progress and become more experienced, you will become more proficient in balancing color, line, pattern, and texture to create a beautiful primitive rug. Design is simply a matter of choice. Don't use everything in equal proportion but concentrate on one or two main elements, subordinating the others to maintain simplicity, the hallmark of primitive rugs.

We must balance pattern in a hooked rug with areas of relief. "Spot" is a relatively solid area of color and pattern against the variety of hit-and-miss stripes in the background and border. This area of calm in a sea of pattern is a necessity. Imagine substituting a Dalmatian in the design. Chaos!

Pattern in rug design can be achieved by a simple subject and busy patterned background, such as "American Trotter," or in an intricately patterned subject and a plain background, such as "Nesting Chickens."

Since shading and intricate detail are not possible with primitive strips, the primitive hooker must rely upon pattern and texture to enliven her rug. She does so with mottled dyeing for water, sky, and objects; mixing and blending shades for grass, trees, and backgrounds; and spot dyeing for leaves, animals, and backgrounds. All these techniques create primitive shading and surface interest that were originally products of the scrap bag but must now be worked out with new material. But do not use these all at once, please!

Since we are not aiming for realism, pattern can be employed in an amusing way. Using various checked material, we can simulate bricks or feathers. Plaids and spot dyeing can be used for foliage. Calico cats can be created from plaids. The primitive rugmakers' divorce from reality gives them free rein to be innovative in the use of materials.

The Texture of Feathers

Because of their humble status in the barnyard (here today, gone on Sunday), chickens have not captured the attention that they deserve from modern rugmakers. The variety of species and plumages, the divergent characteristics of rooster and hen, the appeal of chicks, and the abstract beauty of eggs make a fitting subject for the art of rug hooking.

One of the first known antique rugs to capture this appeal is pictured in *The Index of American Design*, "Fighting Cocks," a handsewn shirred rug on linen dating from the late eighteenth century. Simple chicken rugs (dual images of the fowl) are found in many varieties in early primitive rugs.

Commercial chicken patterns eschewed the lowly barnyard milieu and chose more dramatic moments in poultry life. Crowing at dawn and protecting the chicks from hawks are two of Edward S. Frost's patterns.

The familiarity and simple shape of chickens encouraged amateur rug artists to draw their own designs. The resulting hooked rugs showed a naive and charming interpretation of the barnyard favorite.

Feathers, always a challenge, were handled simply enough with fabric choice—checked work pants. The abundant supply of these worn-out pants also made them a natural choice for borders and backgrounds. The small brown-and-tan checked fabric appears as a filler in hit-and-miss and was overdyed for hen and rooster as well.

Popular chickens of the day, Rhode Island Reds and Plymouth Rocks, lent themselves to home-drawn versions and color choices that were readily available in the ragbag or home dye pot.

The interplay of pattern and texture is perfectly depicted in the pattern "Nesting Chickens." The subjects are a Silver Pencilled Plymouth Rock rooster and hen on a nest. I used twenty-two kinds of checks, tweeds, plaids, and mottled wool in its design. Each feather section is a different texture and pattern created by dyed and patterned wool. Because the breed is black and white and I had a large variety of wool scraps in these tones, I decided to have fun and make every feather area different. Using black-and-white chickens is a simple version of this rug; shades of blue and cranberry make a more sophisticated one. An intricately patterned rug needs simplicity of color.

To keep the color combination "country," the background was mottled in ochre (Old Gold, Nugget Gold, and Golden Brown), but other medium-to-light colors would be equally attractive in the background.

Tiny amounts are needed for the tail feathers. A hem,

pocket, or cuff can make one feather. Ask your local seam-
stress or tailor to save these throwaways for you, or go through
your closet and be ruthless!

My blue-and-cranberry version of this pattern threw realism to the wind, but the resulting combination of Wedgewood
blue, navy, maroon, and cranberry chickens was gorgeous. If
you would like to use natural dyes for the rug, substitute Rhode
Island Reds for Plymouth Rock chickens and vary the feathers
with shades of onion skin dye. *The Standard of Perfection*, the
bible of the poultry business, is an invaluable source for breed
characteristics.

The Textures of Background

Whereas "Nesting Chickens" is a riot of texture in subject
matter, "American Trotter" reverses the field and has a relatively untextured center of interest but a strong textural background. The mottled sky, using undulating hooking, suggests
speed or air currents. Spot dyeing the trees and grass provides
color and pattern in the landscape. The large area of track is
hooked in a subtle hit-and-miss technique, and the soft horizontal rows are hooked in a mixture of tans, beiges, and
browns that produce a strong but subtle foreground.

PATTERN

"Nesting Chickens"

2 by 3 feet

© Pat Hornafius 1990

DYES
(W. Cushing & Co.)

You may not have to dye at all for this rug if you have the appropriate fabrics. Black-and-white and gray-and-white wools are available in yard goods and used clothing (my source). If you are following my dyeing directions, you will need the following dyes:

Terra Cotta

Nugget Gold

Old Gold

Golden Brown

Silver Gray

MATERIALS

Comb and wattle

1 ounce of wool dip dyed in Terra Cotta or 1 ounce of various shades of red.

Feet, beaks, and straw

2 ounces of Nugget Gold or various shades of gold or wool dip dyed in Old Gold.

Eyes

Scrap of black wool for the hen and rooster.
Tiny scrap of peach wool for the chicks.

Rooster

Head and wing. 1 ounce of white wool.
Neck. ½ ounce of large black-and-white check.
Breast and front leg. 2 ounces of black wool.
Rear leg. ½ ounce of charcoal wool.
Back. 2 ounces of small black-and-white checks.
Tail feathers. ½ ounce each of seven combinations of black, white and gray wool:
1. black
2. black-and-white check or border plaid
3. dark gray mottled wool
4. charcoal black (same as the chicks)
5. gray-and-white check
6. gray tweed check
7. dark gray plaid or tweed

Hen

Head. ½ ounce of white wool.
Neck ruff. 1 ounce of gray-and-white checks.
Wing. 2 ounces of dark gray plaid.
Body. 2 ounces of black wool.
Tail feathers. ½ ounce each of 7 shades of black, gray and white wool leftovers from the rooster, hen and dip-dyed grays:
1. dark gray plaid from hen's wing material
2. gray-and-white check from hen's neck material
3. black
4. light gray dip-dyed wool (1 ounce)
5. dark gray
6. black-and-white checks
7. dark gray mottled wool

Chicks

Outline. ½ ounce of charcoal gray wool.
Body. 1 ounce of charcoal black.

Nest

Outline. Several strips of light brown wool.
Nest. 1 ounce of dark camel wool.

Fan corners

3 ounces of red or Terra Cotta–dyed wool.
Outer line and inner corner. 2 ounces of charcoal black.
Gray fan outline. Scraps from rooster's gray tail-feathers' material
(#3).

Background

16 ounces of ochre wool or mottled Old Gold and Golden Brown
wool. I tried to simulate chicken-feed color here, but you can substitute any medium light color.

Ground lines

2 ounces of gray-and-white check overdyed with background
color.

Border

4 ounces of any black-and-white check or plaid material. I had
a perfect black-and-white plaid with hints of green and red
woven in.

Dyeing for "Nesting Chickens"

Dip dyeing is a method of dyeing graduated shades of color on
the same strip of wool. The technique is valuable to primitive
rugmakers and in tapestry rug hooking as well. It can be used
for various shades in a small area, eliminating the need for
changing colors and tiny strips. By hooking a continuous
strand of dip-dyed wool into an area, the work is shaded natu-
rally by degrees. I have talked about mottled dyeing, spot
dyeing, and half-and-half dyeing. Here is another method of
dyeing to create a multishaded effect.

Dip dyeing is as close as primitive rugmakers get to realistic shading. It is also a great way to get three or four shades
on a 45-inch piece of wool for those tiny areas that need
variegation. I save all the ends left over from the long strand
for future use in flowers, leaves, and so on. This dip-dyed wool
can simulate a plaid if hooked over a large area but is particularly useful for a small area. Use only salt as a mordant because vinegar takes up too quickly. Wear gloves to protect
your hands.

Dip Dyeing the Comb and Wattle

Use 1/32 teaspoon of Terra Cotta for 1 ounce of presoaked white
wool. Dissolve the Terra Cotta dye in a small 1-quart pan of
water with ½ teaspoon of salt and simmer. Immerse 15 inches
of the 45-inch strip in the simmering dye bath for the length of

time you need to get a rich Terra Cotta color (about thirty seconds). You are dyeing this wool in three sections. You do not want the last section to become too pale for the wattle.

After the first thirty seconds or so, immerse the second 15-inch section in the dye bath. Hold it there, or drape the remaining length over the pan. Continue simmering the first two sections for thirty more seconds. Drop the last 15-inch section into the dye bath and cover. Simmer the whole piece for thirty minutes before removing. See section II for directions on washing, rinsing, and drying the wool.

This process will give you three graduated shades from dark Terra Cotta to light Terra Cotta. For flowers or leaves, you may want an even more gradual shading and can space your immersions more closely. Please wear gloves and do not breathe in the fumes as you are immersing the wool. You can drape the wool over the edge of the pan as you go, but avoid the burner. Wool scorches against a hot surface.

Dip Dyeing the Legs, Beaks, and Straw
Dissolve 1/32 teaspoon of Old Gold and 2/32 teaspoon of Nugget Gold plus 1 teaspoon of salt in 1 quart of simmering water for 2 ounces of white wool in a 60-inch strip. Old Gold takes up faster than Nugget Gold, so your first immersion will produce a deep dark gold and the last immersion will end up a pale yellow-gold. Follow the timing for graduated immersions (thirty-second intervals) and simmering (thirty minutes) given above for dip-dyeing the comb and wattle. Wash, rinse, and dry the wool.

Decide how many graduations of color you wish for the legs and straw. I used three. You need a dark gold for the tiny beaks, and this first length of 15 inches will produce a gold deep enough to show up against the ochre background. For the legs, I use the medium gold and dark gold against the ochre background. The straw can be all three shades against the camel nest, as there is enough contrast there to define the single lines of straw.

Dip Dyeing the Feathers and Fan Outline
Dissolve 1/32 teaspoon of Silver Gray with 1/4 teaspoon of salt in a 1-quart pan of simmering water. Presoak 1 ounce of white wool, and immerse it in five sections of 12 inches each at

twenty-second intervals. Wash, rinse, and dry the wool. You will get a range of gray from darkest gray to very pale gray. Use the lighter end for the tail feathers and the medium-to-dark sections for the fan outline.

I speckled the lightest gray end with a grain or two of Silver Gray after my dyeing was completed for another mottled color in the rooster's tail. Remove the wool, squeeze out the dye bath (wear gloves), and drape the very pale end over the edge and into the bottom of a 1-quart pan. Do not get the other shades involved here unless you need more darkening. With the greatest of care, sprinkle Silver Gray dye from the tip of a knife one grain at a time over the pale gray surface at intervals. You will get very dark spots, as you are not diluting the dye with water. The water remaining in the wool will disperse the dye particles and cause bleeding. Simmer the wool for several minutes. If you must, add water a little at a time so the pan does not dry out. Too much water will dilute and spread the dye. Cover the pan to hasten take-up and conserve steam. Permit the wool to cool in the pan before washing it.

Dyeing the Hen's Neck Ruff

This dyeing is optional and can be done if you do not have gray-and-white checks for the hen's neck ruff. You can speckle 1 ounce of white wool with Silver Gray as described above for the rooster's tail feathers, but you will need a larger area in which to work. Lay the wet white wool to be dyed in a casserole pan. Sprinkle the wool with a few grains of Silver Gray dye from the tip of a knife, sprinkle with salt, cover, and steam for fifteen minutes in the oven. Do not let the pan run dry. Wash, rinse, and dry the wool.

Dyeing the Background

To dye 16 ounces of white wool and two ounces of gray-and-white checks for ground lines, dissolve 1/32 teaspoon of Old Gold, 1/32 teaspoon of Nugget Gold, and 1/32 teaspoon of Golden Brown plus 1 teaspoon of salt in a 2-gallon dye pot of simmering water. You will want your wool to be very crowded in this kettle to give you the mottling you desire. Add 1/4 cup of vinegar after twenty minutes of simmering.

Drop the presoaked white wool (16 ounces) and gray-and-white checked pieces (2 ounces) into the dye pot, and lift once to expose all the wool. Arrange the wool in even pockets and folds to spot dye a little later.

Simmer $1/32$ teaspoon of Golden Brown in 2 cups of water. When the main dye pot and wool have simmered fifteen minutes, pour the hot dye solution on top of the wool (now ochre). Do not lift or stir. This top dressing will further mottle the ochre wool and give hints of darker areas to the body of the background.

After five minutes of take-up, lift the wool out of the dye pot, pour in ¼ cup of white vinegar, and stir the water before returning the wool to the dye bath. The vinegar will facilitate Nugget Gold take-up, always the last dye to absorb. Continue to simmer for ten more minutes. Wash, rinse, and dry the wool.

Dyeing the Corners

You will have enough gray and dark gray left over from your chickens' tail feathers for the outlines of the fan and fan corners.

To dye 3 ounces of white wool for the terra-cotta fans, use $3/32$ teaspoon of Terra Cotta dye plus ½ teaspoon of salt in a 1-quart dye pot. Simmer the dye, salt, and water to dissolve the particles before immersing the presoaked wool. Salt dulls Terra Cotta; the ½ teaspoon is just enough to permit take-up. Plunge the wool into the dye bath, lifting once to be sure all surfaces are saturated. Cover and simmer for half an hour. If any dye remains in the water, permit the wool to cool in the dye bath for complete take-up. Wash, rinse, and dry the wool.

Hooking "Nesting Chickens"

Before beginning to hook your rug, see "Cutting the Wool" in section II.

Hooking the Rooster's Body

Begin hooking the rooster comb with a dip-dyed Terra Cotta strip. Start with the darkest end and hook the outline of the comb. When the medium red starts to show up, hook around the head and wattle. You will want the lightest end in the very center of the wattle.

Hook in the black eye and outline the eye, head, and wattle with white wool strips. If you have a picture of a Silver Pencilled Plymouth Rock rooster, it will help you with demarcations.

Continue with the neck, hooking vertically in rows the way the feathers would fall. Then hook the wing in black and white. The breast and front leg flow together. Outline the whole section first and continue to fill in, following the contour of the shape. You will find that the wing's black center section will meet the black breast, but your eyes will make the necessary division of space, and the area will not look confused.

Outline the rear leg in charcoal black. If your charcoal is too dark and disappears into the front leg, hook a single line of one of the dark plaids to divide those leg areas. Continue hooking the black-and-white-checked rooster's back, again outlining and following the contour of the body in curved vertical rows.

Hooking the Rooster's Tail

All the wool for the rooster's tail was pulled from other parts of the two chickens. Keep the tail-feather shades alternating between light and dark so that each row of feathers is distinct from the next. Arrange your colors in a dark, medium, and light sequence. Begin with a black feather against the background for maximum contrast. Begin hooking at the tip of the feather, returning to the body and reversing almost to the end before cutting your strip. This method, used for all of the tail feathers, will ensure a pointed tip and eliminate cuts in the strand.

Hooking the Beaks, Legs, and Straw

Hook the very darkest gold for the rooster, hen, and chicks' beaks, again beginning with the tip. For the rooster, start the legs at the outermost claw with the darkest gold for definition against the background. Hook up along the edge of one leg, reverse, and hook down the other side. Save the lighter shades for the third row in the center. Again, begin at the claw and hook up the middle. Add spurs and other claws with separate strips.

You can use the lighter shades of gold for the beaks and

legs of the chicks. These shades will show up against the camel-colored nest.

For the single rows of straw, use the remaining small pieces from the gold dip-dyed strips. Use the darkest golds against the background and the lightest shades against the hen and nest.

Hooking the Hen's Body

As with the rooster, hook in the outline of the comb and wattle with the darkest section of terra cotta before filling in the center with the lighter shades.

Hook the hen's head with white, being sure to keep the points of the feathers sharp. Now outline and fill in the neck in gray-and-white checks. Hook in the wing, following the contour. Hook the back of the hen and under the wing in black.

Hooking the Hen's Tail

Each feather is a different fabric of black and white or gray. Use leftover strips from the hen and rooster. Be sure to alternate light, medium, and dark throughout the tail. I used more gray feathers in my hen's tail than in my rooster's to vary the design and pick up the hen's gray neck tones.

Hooking the Chicks and the Nest

Outline the chicks in a light charcoal gray and hook in their bodies with a charcoal black or dark charcoal gray. Hook the eyes in a color not already used in the rug. I like peach or another unobtrusive color. You have already hooked the feet and beaks in gold and the straw in a mixed variety of golds.

Outline the nest with the dark camel. I run a row of light brown under the rim and make several vertical lines with light brown in the nest as well. Hook the camel nest in vertical rows and the rim in horizontal rows for variety and ease of hooking. It is difficult to hook around those droopy straws, but get in there even if you must cross over the single row of straw gold.

Hooking the Background

You are now ready to hook the background, but first put in one or two rows of the fan outlines to delineate the shape and one row of background wool to outline the outside edge. Outline all the subject matter—hen, nest, and rooster—with the background color. Using the overdyed checks, hook in the lines indicating the ground and your initials in a bottom corner. Begin hooking the background, following the undulating lines you have dashed in on your pattern with a permanent marking pen.

If your wool is sufficiently mottled, you can begin hooking in long strips and get the benefit of a variegated background without changing colors. This approach is easy and fast.

Hook in the background, bumping against the border edges and turning your strips before cutting. Scatter your various cuts in the body of the rug so they do not end up in one place.

Hooking the Border

To stabilize the corners before hooking the fans, hook the five rows of border. Do not stop and start at the same place, but stagger your rows so the end cuts will not appear in the same spot. To turn and maintain a sharp corner, hook one loop past the previous row, then turn and go up the side. Two sideways loops equal one frontward loop.

Fill in the already-outlined terra-cotta fans, leaving the oval openings for the background color. Your rug is now complete. See section VIII for hemming and binding instructions.

PATTERN ──────────────────────────────────────

"American Trotter"

23 by 37 inches

MATERIALS

Blinders, whip, wheel rim, details on driver (eye, moustache, shoe, hair)

Scraps of black wool.

Skin tones for the face and hands of the driver

Scraps of peach wool.

Hat, coat, harness, traces, seat, wheel tire, bridle, and reins

2 ounces of shades of red wool or wool dyed Egyptian Red.

Collar, cuffs, and hooves

Scraps of white wool.

Pants and hat section

1 ounce of light camel wool.

Hub, girth, and studs

½ ounce of gold wool.

Horse

Body. 4 ounces of shades of dark brown wool or wool dyed Seal Brown.
Mane, tail, and rear legs. 1 ounce of dark gray flannel dyed Seal Brown.

Track

8 ounces of four shades of beige, off-white, taupe, and tan wool.

Grass

6 ounces of three or four shades of medium to dark green wool.

Sky

8 ounces of shades of light blue wool or mottled Williamsburg-dyed wool.

Border

6 ounces of brown, blue, and taupe plaids, checks, or tweeds.

DYES
(W. Cushing & Co.)

Egyptian Red

Copenhagen Blue

Golden Brown

Reseda Green

Silver Gray

Gold

Seal Brown or black walnut dye

Robin's Egg Blue

Dark Green

Khaki Drab

The Rug Design

"American Trotter" is an adaptation of *Harry Wilkes*, a Currier & Ives lithograph (#518) printed in 1885. This famous trotter was driven by Frank Van Ness in record time. Harness racing, a popular sport of the late 1800s, was the subject of many Currier & Ives lithographs.

The textural pattern of this rug remains in the background; the horse and driver are plain fabrics showing only highlights. A mottled blue sky, dyed in the scrunch style, as well as various greens for the grass and tree forms and a variety of taupes, beiges, and tans for the track create the necessary balance between plain and patterned. "Let Her Go," the cry for speed, was added to the foreground for interest and color.

The horse could be made without the driver, sulky, or harness and be a wonderfully vigorous design by itself. The running horse was a popular tradition in hooked-rug design, generally copied from a calendar, weathervane, or print. I have seen this running horse hooked in dark brown against a background of hit-and-miss in a medley of colors. The undulating horizontal hooking showed speed and excitement in the flow of the line and the bright colors, adding all the pattern and textural interest necessary without the sky, grass, and track.

If you wish to keep the background relatively simple—shades of mixed camel wools are nice—make an interesting border. Colorful chevrons, using lots of solid red and brown with multicolored checks and plaids, are an authentic antique border for a horse design. The vigor of the border complements the motion of the horse.

Dyeing for "American Trotter"

You may not need to dye every ounce of wool required for this rug. The small amounts needed for flesh, black, gold, and white should be available in scraps or used clothing. I found my shades of green in pleated skirts and a wool suit (circa 1950) that I overdyed with Reseda Green. I will give you formulas for dyeing each shade from scratch, but here is a chance to overdye, spot dye, and dye half-and-half for the small amounts required. Use up small pieces of light plaids, checks, and tweeds that may need a color boost. You are dyeing such small amounts that you can experiment and have some fun.

I used black walnut dye full strength for the horse and mane. This warm authentic antique color lends a look to our Currier & Ives design that commercial dyes cannot match, but if walnut shells are not available to you, you can substitute Seal Brown. I dyed the horse with white wool and used gray flannel for the dark areas: mane, tail, and rear legs. The fabrics can all be dyed in the same dye pot if you are using walnut dye or in separate dye pots if you are using Seal Brown.

For the track I obtained two light shades of walnut from the dye solution that remained after I dyed the horse; the darker tone was immersed longer. A series of shades from taupe to light bone can be dyed in this depleted black-walnut dye bath, giving the ever lighter shades needed for the road.

If you cannot dye with walnuts, gather a number of pale beiges, tans, taupes, and bone wools to mix and blend in your track area. Since this is really a hit-and-miss type of hooking, very small strips can be used.

Shades of red can be found for the tack and driver's coat if you do not plan to dye. You need only a small quantity. To get a lighter red for the driver's sleeve (necessary to delineate the arm), simmer a small piece of red wool with one tablespoon of mild detergent to take out some of the dye. This lightening process usually works with red cloth, as it is so heavily dyed. Use the slightly lighter shade for the cap visor, sleeve, and rein ring to define the forms. I chose this horse and these driver silks to duplicate the colors of Harry Wilkes and his driver. The Hall of Fame of the Trotter in Goshen, New York, was very helpful to me in planning the colors, but you need not be so authentic. Create your own trotter with brilliant silks, and be original!

Dyeing the Reds

To dye 1 ounce of medium red wool and 1 ounce of slightly lighter red wool, use two 1-ounce white wool strips and the following formula.

Dissolve $2/32$ teaspoon of Egyptian Red plus ½ teaspoon of salt in 1 quart of boiling water. Immerse the first presoaked strip in the simmering dye bath, count to thirty, and immerse the other presoaked strip. Simmer for half an hour. Permit the wool to cool in the dye bath for complete take-up. See section II for directions on washing, rinsing, and drying the wool.

To dip dye a 2-ounce strip, immerse one end for thirty seconds and then drop in the other half for 15 inches of dark red and 15 inches of medium red on the same piece. Simmer for half an hour. Wash, rinse, and dry the wool. For more information on dip dyeing, see the dyeing directions for the pattern "Nesting Chickens."

Dyeing the Camel Color
You need 1 ounce of camel wool for the driver's pants and cap. Use 1/64 teaspoon of Golden Brown dye in 1 quart of water plus ½ teaspoon of salt for your dye bath. Immerse the 1-ounce piece of wool and simmer for fifteen minutes. Wash, rinse, and dry the wool. This dyeing process produces a pleasant warm camel color, but substitute a light camel wool if you have it. Mix any leftover camel wool into the track.

Dyeing the Flesh Color
If you need to dye a peach color for the face and hand of the driver, use an 8-inch scrap of white, off-white, or very light beige wool and tint it with a few grains of Egyptian Red dye. This dye makes light pink on white and a more swarthy look on beige wool. Again, put the dye in one quart of boiling water with ½ teaspoon of salt and simmer for fifteen minutes. Wash, rinse, and dry the wool.

Dyeing the Gold Color
Put 1/32 teaspoon of Gold plus ¼ teaspoon of salt in 1 quart of boiling water for half an hour to dye the ½ ounce of wool needed for the tack. Wash, rinse, and dry the wool. You can make the wheel hub gold as well, or use a strip of gray flannel.

Dyeing the Horse
Dye the wool for the horse's body in a black walnut dye bath (see section III, "Making Brown Dye from Walnuts"), or use Seal Brown dye. For 4 ounces of white wool, use ¼ teaspoon of Seal Brown, 1 teaspoon of salt, and ¼ cup of white vinegar in 2 quarts of simmering water. Take-up will be rapid: you want variegation for your shiny horse. When you cut your wool into

strips, save the light areas that appear for the glossy lines in the horse's coat. Immerse the presoaked wool all at once in the dye bath and simmer half an hour. Wash, rinse, and dry the wool.

To dye the darker brown needed for the horse's mane, tail, and rear leg, use $2/32$ teaspoon of Seal Brown dye plus $\frac{1}{2}$ teaspoon of salt and 1 tablespoon of vinegar in a 1-quart pan to overdye 1 ounce of gray flannel. If you do not have gray flannel, which will automatically produce a darker tone, use 1 ounce of white wool, double the required Seal Brown dye to $4/32$ teaspoon, and dye in a simmering bath for half an hour. Permit the wool to cool in the dye bath for complete take-up. Wash, rinse, and dry the wool.

Dyeing the Track

If you have used black walnut dye for the horse and mane, the dye solution remaining will make a lovely taupe or light brown. I continued using the depleting walnut dye, adding more white wool strips and water plus $\frac{1}{4}$ cup of vinegar, to dye the tan shades in the track. Because I wanted the road to be light overall, I saved 4 ounces of the wool for the lightest dye bath of walnut, resulting in a bone shade. This color planning is similar to the hit-and-miss background for "Spot."

If you plan to use commercial dye, begin with four 1-ounce strips of white wool to $1/32$ teaspoon of Seal Brown and 1 teaspoon of salt (for slow take-up). Simmer the dye and salt in 2 quarts of water. You will be immersing individual strips every three minutes until all the strips are used and the dye bath is depleted. Permit all four strips to remain in the dye bath, and simmer ten more minutes. Wash, rinse, and dry the wool.

To dye the remaining 4 ounces of white wool for the road, dissolve $1/32$ teaspoon of Seal Brown and $\frac{1}{2}$ teaspoon of salt in 2 quarts of simmering water. Immerse the presoaked wool all at once and simmer in a crowded fashion for a mottled look. After ten minutes, add $\frac{1}{4}$ cup of white vinegar for complete take-up. Continue to simmer twenty more minutes. Wash, rinse, and dry the wool. The colors from the two 4-ounce pieces of Seal Brown will be blended for a harmonious whole. Plan to add other shades of tan, beige, and camel to enliven the track.

Dyeing the Landscape

If you have leftover green fabric scraps, use them here for a variegated textural background. I like to mix plaids, checks, tweeds, and stripes for this type of landscape. Three or four values of color also help to define low trees, shrubs, and grasses.

Light green. Use $1/64$ teaspoon of Reseda Green and $1/64$ teaspoon of Gold plus $1/4$ teaspoon of salt in 1 quart of hot water. Immerse your 2 ounces of white wool and simmer for half an hour. Wash, rinse, and dry the wool. This process will give you a light olive green.

Medium green. Use $1/32$ teaspoon of Reseda Green plus $1/2$ teaspoon of salt in 1 quart of hot water. Immerse the 2-ounce white wool strip and simmer for half an hour. Wash, rinse, and dry the wool.

Dark green. Use $1/32$ teaspoon of Dark Green and $1/32$ teaspoon of Reseda Green plus 1 teaspoon of salt in 1 quart of hot water. Immerse your 2 ounces and simmer for half an hour. Add 1 tablespoon of vinegar after fifteen minutes and continue simmering. Wash, rinse, and dry the wool.

If you have light green or neutral plaids or checks, drop them into the dye bath with the required ounces. In this way, you will have more shades with textured wools to add variety to your landscape. Use the darker textured material for trees and the medium shades for grass.

Dyeing the Sky

The sky area is gently mottled and serves as a contrast to the straight hit-and-miss track and variegated landscape. You want to mottle the wool to produce shades of very light blue to medium blue. A solid-colored sky looks like a rainy day—dismal.

For 8 ounces of white wool, use the following formula:

$3/32$ teaspoon of Copenhagen Blue

$2/32$ teaspoon of Robin's Egg Blue

$1/64$ teaspoon of Khaki Drab

$1/64$ teaspoon of Silver Gray

1 tablespoon of salt and $1/4$ cup of white vinegar

Simmer the dye and mordants. Immerse the presoaked wool all at once, lift to expose the wool, stir slightly, and cover.

Simmer for half an hour. Permit the wool to cool in the dye bath for complete take-up. Wash, rinse, and dry the wool.

Dyeing the Border

You may want to overdye the border plaid if you cannot find blue, tan, and brown plaids. I frequently overdye neutral plaids and tweeds to gain the extra color needed to tie in the border with the color scheme of the rug.

If you have tan-and-brown fabric, overdye it in a weak solution of the sky blue. For 6 ounces of plaid, use $2/32$ teaspoon of Copenhagen Blue and $1/32$ teaspoon of Robin's Egg Blue. Skip the other two dye colors (Khaki Drab and Silver Gray), which drab and soften the blues. Your neutral plaid is already dull enough. Simmer the dye with 1 teaspoon of salt and ¼ cup of white vinegar. You want a fast take-up to prevent your plaid or tweeds from bleeding into the dyebath and mud-dying all your colors. Immerse your presoaked wool and simmer for fifteen minutes. You may have areas undyed because of the fast take-up. Good! They will further enhance the border. Wash, rinse, and dry the wool.

Hooking "American Trotter"

Before beginning to hook your rug, see "Cutting the Wool" in section II.

Hooking the Sulky and Driver

Hook the areas closest to the viewer first. We have not had much overlapping in my primitive rug designs, as this visual concept is more sophisticated than most country rugs display. Begin with the wheel hub. Hook the black rim and the black spokes. Hook closely, skipping only one mesh for these lines to keep them well defined. Hook the red rubber tire next. Use a light Egyptian Red for the tires. Think of rubber-eraser red. It will be a shade lighter than the driver's coat.

Hook the driver next. Put in the tiny black eye, moustache, hairline, and velvet lapel. Now fill in the face, defining the nose and chin. Hook one row of white for the collar and cuffs. Hook the hand with flesh-colored wool. Hook the visor. Use a lighter shade of red to distinguish it from the rest of the cap. Finish the cap in darker red. The short jacket is dark red, and the sleeve is light red. Use light camel for the middle section in the cap and the driver's trousers. I used a tiny scrap of light Seal Brown wool for the soles of the black shoes after I hooked the traces and seat in two shades of red.

To hook the tack, first hook two rows of gold for the girth. Use black, gold, and light red for the rein ring and darker red for the reins. The bridle is also dark red, and the studs are gold.

Hooking the Horse

Hook the blinders and whip in black. Again, hook closely to define the shapes. Make the nostril light red to denote a speeding horse. Use white or off-white for the hooves. The rear legs, mane, and tail are dark brown, as is the forelock. Hook in these areas before beginning the body of the horse.

Use your pale brown in single short rows to indicate musculature and gloss on the horse's coat. Hook the outline of the body, and following the contours, fill in the horse. If your brown wool is mottled, it will enhance the beauty of the horse's coat.

Hooking the Track

Your hit-and-miss shades of wool are dyed and cut. Place the deeper shades in one bag and the lightest bone or beige shades in another bag. You will want to use twice as much lighter wool as darker shades to keep the track light in tone. When you hook the track, use two light strips to each dark strip. Use the deepest tan or light brown for your initials and the date. If you choose to include the words "Let Her Go!", hook these letters now with your darkest shade of red.

Outline the entire track area with the lightest beige. Keep the lines straight at the border edge and across the upper edge of the track. Dash in several straight lines on your foundation here and there to aid you when hooking the flat hit-and-miss track.

Use the darkest values under the hooves so they will not get lost in the dust. Now start hooking horizontally, choosing at random from your many shades of tan. Do not cut off the ends when you hook inside the spokes but turn and cut somewhere in the center. Be sure to continue the same color to the next spoke; the line should be continuous and not chopped off like wedges of cheese. Remember to alternate light and dark strips two to one.

Hooking the Landscape

To keep your rug perfectly even, hook in one border row around the entire rug. It is difficult to outline the landscape, since you are creating rows of trees, shrubs, and grass and no single color predominates. Instead, using the border row as your starting and stopping place, hook in a line of bumpy shrubs with the shades of darkest green at the edge of the track. This darker area will define the track and lend interest to the background. Make a row of bumpy trees at the horizon. Again, use your deepest greens to define the line against the blue sky. Picking and choosing, hook horizontal lines of grass with various medium and light shades, using several rows of each before changing colors. This technique will avoid another hit-and-miss area in the middle ground, detracting from the horse and driver. Having completed the landscape, move to the sky.

Hooking the Sky

You should have a nice mottled piece of blue ready to hook for the sky. The mottling has taken care of clouds, sunshine, and shadow. Dash in directional hooking lines with a permanent marking pen, moving around your subject matter in an undulating fashion to simulate air currents. Outline the entire sky and fill it in.

Hooking the Border

Complete the border rows. The plaid fabric has quite enough interest considering the complexity of the rest of the rug. Adding a fancy border here would be distracting. If, however, you wish to make the rug much larger, increase the background and place a rainbow arching over the horse and sulky for luck, using a strip of grass in the foreground. I've seen this version hooked with very large four-leaf clovers in the bottom grass strip for more good luck.

To finish your rug, follow the directions in section VIII.

VII

Primitive
Still Lifes

Primitive still lifes are just that—primitive. Untrained artists did the best they could. Their flowers resemble nothing in nature but hark back to the earlier crewel flower forms, simplifying them greatly along the way. Tambour workers of the late eighteenth century to the midnineteenth century created crewel flowers and leaf forms on fine fabric through a procedure much like a miniature version of rug hooking. Material was held taut in an embroidery hoop, and the hooker used a tiny crochet hook to pull a loop of thread to the surface of the fabric, creating a chain stitch. This fine so-called hooking reached its zenith around 1800 and then declined when machine-made embroidery became available in 1840. It was then that rug hooking took hold. Perhaps the legacy of tambour was the hand-hooked rug.

Color Schemes

Balancing the many colors in a flower bouquet is essential. You will notice the rather awkward flower arrangement of "Antique Flower Basket," which repeats only two of each variety, with the exception of three blue daisies. Primitive rugmakers did not know that an uneven number of motifs made for good design. The pale to deep colors of the flowers repeated in the rug, however, create large blocks of pink throughout the design. Notice that the huge roses are in opposite corners, the blue flowers are central, and the palest carnations are in the middle. Tulips, posies, and grapes in middle tones flirt around the edges. This arrangement draws the eye to the center of the rug, then out to the edges.

The dark, medium, and light leaves alternate throughout the design. Primitive rugmakers hated repetition, so changing each leaf slightly not only provided contrasts where needed (against light and medium flowers) but also made hooking more fun and creative.

Borders for Still Lifes

Because of their complexity, flower bouquets do not need fancy borders. Plain rows of hooking do well for this type of design, either in solid colors that pick up a color in the rug or in hit-and-miss choices that use scraps from the center.

To extend the size of the rug without increasing the size of the bouquet (four-foot bouquets can be rather overwhelming), you can scatter the flower forms throughout a solid-colored border. Connected by vines and tendrils, these simple small flowers pick up rug colors and echo the designs in the rug center.

Commercial designs balance and repeat the border devices. Not so with hand-drawn primitive rugs. The border flowers, connected with stems, allowed the country rugmaker another area for change and variation. Sometimes a bird or bee was included. Grapes decorated one edge of a primitive flower rug, appearing nowhere else in the composition.

Use your imagination, have fun, change, add, and delete to your heart's content. Formality is not at work here. Only remember to repeat your colors for a harmonious whole.

A great variety of colors were employed for flowers and leaves. Natural dyes, soft to begin with, faded in time and rendered the colors closely related in value. Although rugmakers, like crewel workers, included many shades of color for each flower and leaf, realistic shading was not attempted. Rather, color was used for delineation of parts: center, petals, and leaves.

Flowers

Concentric rows of colors radiated from large, round centers. Rows of petals were defined by lighter or darker outlines. Realism played no part in color selections. Flowers were divided into many colored sections to provide contrast to adjacent shapes.

No attempt was made to depict the correct number of petals in the daisies or duplicate their color. Closely related colors were used for outline and petal shapes.

Flower forms were exaggerated and fanciful. One can only guess at their origins.

Alternating light and dark crescent-shaped sections imitated the enfolding petals of a rose.

Pinwheels, flowers alternating light and dark ellipses, resembled the opening petals of a rose.

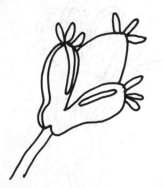

Buds were rendered in a recognizable form, complete with pod, sepals, and stamens, as they are so simple in shape.

Roses

These imaginative flower forms were abstractions of the real thing. "Antique Flower Basket" depicts roses with exaggerated dark spiraling centers, light frills, center pods, and undulating petals. These spectacular roses make no attempt at realism in shape or shading, but we recognize them immediately.

Saucer-shaped flowers resembled wheel cogs. Bands of concentric colors radiated from the center in various shades unrelated to actual flower petals.

Asters and Dahlias

Asters and dahlias were depicted in side view, their few but enormous petals adorned with giant stamens and pistils in many different colors. Huge sepals also decorated the flowers, attached to fat and sturdy stems trailing individually throughout the arrangement. Since primitive art rarely used overlapping, each stem, leaf, and flower stood by itself, clearly outlined in the background.

Tulips

Tulips, favored holdovers from crewel design, were transformed by color division and many petals. Originally from Asia Minor, tulips gained great value in seventeenth-century Holland, causing "tulipomania" and an ensuing financial crash. The motif remained in English crewelwork, no doubt influenced by the East Indian imported cotton hangings known as palampores, and finally were hooked into humble country rugs.

Carnations

Carnations, generally shown in side view, were also borrowed from crewel design. Individual petals emerged from large sepals. The many petals overlapped in front view, divided from each other by an outline of color.

Fruits

No design was complete without berries, cherries, or grapes. These small rounded forms added needed lightness to the arrangement, much as baby's breath does to our present-day bouquets.

Leaves

The two sides of the leaf, divided by strong-colored veins, were often of colors adjacent on the color wheel. Green was most often employed, but blues, ochres, and combinations of the three were used as well to lend variety and interest. Each leaf in the composition also varied slightly, adding a playful air to the bouquet.

Flower Containers

The type of containers used for bouquets can place the rug design in time. Early designs featured wire or pierced baskets. Victorian work used fancy vases, sometimes with pedestals, and intertwined wicker baskets with or without handles. The humble pot was frequently used in country rugs for "growing" plants.

Giant leaves, resembling king-size fronds, provided an area for color graduation. Half-dark, half-light leaves, leaves shading from dark to light, and prominent veins all gave the rugmakers an opportunity for expressive use of color.

PATTERN

"Antique Flower Basket"

37½ by 26 inches

MATERIALS

Basket

Outline. 3 ounces of black wool.
Inside. 1 ounce of dark oatmeal wool or wool with the medium background color.

Blue Flowers

2 ounces of blue wool.
Outline. ½ ounce of darker blue wool.

Flower stems and veins

2 ounces of bright green plaid.

Grapes

1 ounce each of two shades of mauve wool.

Grape stems

1 ounce of dark brown plaid.

Carnations

1 ounce each of three shades of light pink wool.
Outline. Rosy-pink material from the border line.

Posies

1 ounce of wool dyed dark Terra Cotta and leftover scraps from the other flowers.

Roses

2 ounces each of three shades of wool dyed Terra Cotta.

Gold accents (flower centers, stamens, and rose outlines)

½ ounce each of two shades
of gold wool.

Tulips

Use Terra Cotta–dyed wool leftovers from the roses and posies and Olive Green–dyed wool leftovers from the leaves and stems.

Leaves

3 ounces each of seven shades of Olive Green from very light to very dark.

Background

12 ounces of light oatmeal wool.
6 ounces of medium oatmeal wool.

Border

4 ounces of light green wool.
2 ounces of medium rosy-pink wool.
6 ounces of wool dyed Dark Green.

DYES

(W. Cushing & Co.)

Copenhagen Blue
Robin's Egg Blue
Silver Gray
Khaki Drab
Old Gold
Nugget Gold
Terra Cotta
Olive Green
Bright Green
Reseda Green
Bronze Green
Dark Green
Golden Brown (optional)
Purple (optional)

© Pat Hornafius 1990

Dyeing for "Antique Flower Basket"

I used all my mistakes! A year of disastrous dyeing errors paid off with "Antique Flower Basket," proof that a rug hooker must never throw any wool away. All the wool I had made too dull with complementary colors went into this rug. Although it glows with color, every tone is mellow and aged, giving the rug an air of antiquity. If you are not dyeing all your shades, be sure none of them are too new looking. Throw them down on your oatmeal background before cutting to see if they are suitable. Age them by overdyeing if necessary.

Never begin any rug without laying out the color scheme of fabrics on the background fabric. It is difficult to gauge the color in this rug because of the middle-tone background. A middle tone robs contrasts of color. That's why my dark olives are very dark and my pinks very light.

For the veins and stems, I used up bits and pieces of hideous brown-and-yellow plaids, bright rust-and-white herringbone, and white, lavender, and pink windowpane check. "Uglies" are available at flea markets and thrift shops, as no one else wants them. All these odious shades were overdyed with Olive Green or Golden Brown. The bright undertones of the fabrics spark the single rows needed for these small areas.

A collection of gray tweeds too boring to use elsewhere was overdyed with Dark Green dye solution to work into the leaves and complete the outer border. Always carry out one of the colors in the body of the rug to the border. In this case, a small amount of overdyed gray for leaves was used in a large area of the border. I balanced out the larger area of lighter medium green in the leaves with a small band in the border.

Dyeing the Blue Flowers

The blue flowers with darker edges use the following formula for 2 ounces of wool, plus another ½ ounce for the outlines:

$\frac{1}{32}$ teaspoon of Copenhagen Blue

$\frac{1}{64}$ teaspoon of Robin's Egg Blue

$\frac{1}{128}$ teaspoon of Silver Gray

$\frac{1}{128}$ teaspoon of Khaki Drab

½ teaspoon of salt

Simmer the dye solution with the salt in 1 quart of water until dissolved. Drop the presoaked ½-ounce strip of wool into the initial dye bath, count to twenty, and then immerse the presoaked 2-ounce strip. Simmer both strips for half an hour. If the Robin's Egg Blue dye has not taken up within fifteen minutes, add ¼ cup of white vinegar for the last five minutes. It is a difficult color for take-up. See section II for directions on washing, rinsing, and drying the wool.

If you have a medium-blue piece of wool, you can dull it with $1/128$ teaspoon of Khaki Drab and $1/128$ teaspoon of Silver Grey. Dissolve both dyes and ½ teaspoon of salt in one quart of water. Simmer the dye and immerse the presoaked blue wool all at once. Simmer for half an hour. The deeper blue outline you also need can be dulled in this same formula. Wash, rinse, and dry the wool.

Dyeing the Flower Stems

I had a perfect brown-and-green plaid for the stems, dark enough to show up against the oatmeal background. If you must dye stems, choose a brown, beige, and something-else plaid (2 ounces) and use the following formula:

$1/32$ teaspoon of Bright Green

½ teaspoon of salt

1 tablespoon of white vinegar

Dissolve your ingredients in a one-quart dye pot and immerse your presoaked wool. Simmer only fifteen minutes; plaids may bleed. Wash, rinse, and dry the wool. This vibrant color will add punch to your lighter areas of plaid and provide the needed highlights on your dark plaid.

Dyeing the Grapes

I had two lovely old shades of mauve lavender for the grapes—not too cool, but more to the warm tones. There are several ways to get the mauve wool you need for the grapes.

1. Do not cut all your blue wool for the flowers and pods of the posies. Finish hooking the blue flowers, and use the remaining wool to overdye the two grape mauves, using $1/128$ teaspoon of Purple dye. Wash, rinse, and dry the wool.

2. Remember your color wheel? Blue and red make purple. The leftover uncut scraps of light carnation pink and three medium rose pinks (Terra Cotta–dyed) can be overdyed for a large variety of mauve to lavender grapes. Overdye about

1 ounce of all these leftovers in a dye solution of $1/64$ teaspoon of Copenhagen Blue plus ½ teaspoon of salt in a 1-quart dye bath. Copenhagen Blue by itself is a cold blue. Combining the shades of Terra Cotta (warm) and Copenhagen Blue will produce many shades from cool blue lavender to warm red mauve. Remove the lighter pinks (now blue lavenders) when they reach the intensity desired. The deeper pinks, which will turn mauve, should be left in the dye bath longer. The middle pinks are the control color, a true mauve-lavender. Small amounts need to be simmered for only fifteen minutes. Add 1 tablespoon of white vinegar in the last five minutes of simmering for take-up. Wash, rinse, and dry the wool.

For grape stems, use another scrap of brown plaid or the flower stem material.

Dyeing the Golds

Golds are needed for the flower centers, stamens, and outlines of the roses. For a dull gold, I used $1/64$ teaspoon of Old Gold to ½ ounce of presoaked white wool. Add ½ teaspoon of salt and your dye to a 1-quart dye pot. Again simmer the dye bath and immerse the wool. After take-up, wash, rinse, and dry the wool.

For the brighter flower centers and stamens, use ½ ounce of white wool, $1/64$ teaspoon of Old Gold, and $1/32$ teaspoon of Nugget Gold. Add 1 tablespoon of white vinegar to complete the Nugget Gold take-up in the final five minutes of a fifteen-minute maturing time. Wash, rinse, and dry the wool.

If you have small scraps of yellow wool, overdye the rose outlines with $1/64$ teaspoon of Old Gold, which will effectively dull the original color. To bring the gold down to an even dimmer shade, a grain of Khaki Drab (a greeny drabbing color) will do the job. Test first for color: one tiny snip will tell the story. Failures can be used for the spots in the lower rose.

Dyeing the Carnations

The six sections for each carnation take three shades (two sections of each), plus the darker outline. Presoak the three 1-ounce strips, and dye all of them at once in $1/128$ teaspoon of Terra Cotta plus ½ teaspoon of salt in a 1-quart pan of simmering water. You will want to crowd the pan to encourage mottled dyeing. Count to ten and remove one of the strips. Count to ten again and remove the second strip. Leave the last strip in the dye bath for another ten minutes of simmering. Do not wash these strips as they emerge from the dye bath—there is more dyeing to come.

After a ten-minute simmer for the remaining third strip, the dye should be taken up. Remove this third strip and add one grain of Khaki Drab to the remaining water. Put in the second strip; this overdyeing procedure will slightly dull it. Simmer the second strip gently for ten more minutes and then wash, rinse, and dry all the strips.

You should have a strip of pale pink (#1), a strip of darker pink (#2), and a strip of dulled pink (#3). The rosy-pink outline will be dyed with the rosy-pink line in the border.

Dyeing the Posies

The posies use many shades of gold, pink, and blue and a dark value of Terra Cotta. Use 1 ounce of white wool and several small scraps of beige or tan wool (for the four posy petals). The deep Terra Cotta dye will be used on white wool for the posy stamens, rose spirals, one rose bowl outline, and one row in the tulip petals. We are dyeing this small amount of wool all at once.

For 1 ounce (plus the several tan scraps) of presoaked wool, use $3/32$ teaspoon of Terra Cotta plus ½ teaspoon of salt in 1 quart of water. Simmer for ten minutes before adding 2 tablespoons of white vinegar. This is a heavy dye solution, so permit the wool to cool in the dye bath for complete take-up. Wash, rinse, and dry the wool.

The pod will be two shades of leftover flower blue. No. 2 rose pink will be used for the petal outlines. No. 1 rose pink will be used for the inside of the petals. If you have leftover carnation pinks, you can tint any of these shades with a cup of strong tea for another subtle color change. Try to get as many shades of pink as possible in the rug for interest and variety.

Dyeing the Roses

You will need three shades of Terra Cotta for the roses, plus Old Gold, dark Terra Cotta, and a leftover strip of carnation pink. To obtain the three shades of Terra Cotta (2 ounces each), dye with the following formulas. In each case, add ½ teaspoon of salt to a quart of water in the 1-quart dyepot. Simmer your

2 ounces of presoaked white wool in individual dye pots for thirty minutes. Permit the wool to cool in the dye bath for complete take-up. Wash, rinse, and dry the wool.

1. Light rose. Use $1/64$ teaspoon of Terra Cotta.

2. Medium rose (also used as the rosy-red line in the border). Use $1/32$ teaspoon of Terra Cotta.

3. Dark rose. Use $3/64$ teaspoon of Terra Cotta.

The Tulips

As you are using leftovers from the roses and posies for this flower, no dyeing directions are needed. The center petals of your tulips are leftovers from the leaves and stems.

Dyeing the Large Leaves

You will need seven shades (3 ounces each) of white wool dyed Olive Green and some plaids, tweeds, and checks for the large leaves. The individual dye formulas are given below. Each can be dyed in a 1-gallon pan for a mottled appearance. Add one teaspoon of salt for every 3 ounces of wool. For each dyeing process, immerse the 3 ounces of presoaked material and simmer it in the dye bath for thirty minutes. Permit the wool to cool in the dye bath for complete take-up. Wash, rinse, and dry the wool.

1. Lightest green. Use $1/32$ teaspoon of Olive Green for 3 ounces of white wool.

2. Light green. Use $1/64$ teaspoon of Olive Green and $1/128$ teaspoon of Reseda Green for 3 ounces of white wool.

3. Medium green. Use $1/32$ teaspoon of Reseda Green and $2/32$ teaspoon of Nugget Gold for 3 ounces of light neutral checks, tweeds, or plaids.

4. Dark medium green. Use $2/32$ teaspoon of Bronze Green for 3 ounces of light neutral checks, tweeds, or plaids.

5. Medium dark green. Use $2/32$ teaspoon of Reseda Green on gray tweeds, plaids, or herringbone.

6. Dark green. Use $2/32$ teaspoon of Reseda Green, $2/32$ teaspoon of Dark Green, $1/32$ teaspoon of Bright Green, and $2/32$ teaspoon of Bronze Green for 3 ounces of white wool. Add $1/4$ cup of vinegar after simmering for fifteen minutes and continue simmering for the full half-hour. Allow the wool to cool in the dye bath for complete take-up.

7. Very dark green. Use $^3/_{32}$ teaspoon of Dark Green, $^3/_{32}$ teaspoon of Reseda Green, $^1/_{32}$ teaspoon of Bright Green, and $^3/_{32}$ teaspoon of Bronze Green for 3 ounces of white wool. Add ¼ cup of vinegar after fifteen minutes and continue to simmer fifteen minutes more. Permit the wool to cool in the dye-bath for complete takeup.

Substitute shades of olive green if you have them in used clothing or new fabrics. Primitive rugmakers did not use graduated shades of a single color, as many shades were not available to them and sophisticated dyeing methods were unknown. Rather, they chose the odd shades of olive green from their available hoard of fabrics.

Shading the Background

I hope you can find oatmeal wool from new or used sources. I like the effortless (well, almost effortless) simplicity of the mottled tone.

Do not substitute oatmeal for all the wools dyed for this rug. It does lend an old dirty look to the finished product, but my dye formulas have been devised for white or textured wools, not oatmeal tan. You want to create a sparkle of old colors that is not possible to obtain if you start with oatmeal wool.

For my first "Antique Flower Basket" rug, I used a variety of shades of oatmeal gleaned from years of saving leftovers. For the rug pictured here, however, I tinted a third of the oatmeal wool with spent onion skins from a previous dyeing project. Using the casserole-dyeing method, fold 6 ounces of presoaked oatmeal wool in several layers in a baking pan and sprinkle with semi-spent onion skins and salt. Add 1 inch of water, cover, and bake on warm or simmer for one hour. Cool in the pan. Wash, rinse, and dry the wool. Section II, "Spot Dyeing with Onion Skins in a Casserole," gives more complete instructions on casserole dyeing.

Two shades of oatmeal were used to hook my background. I outlined the entire bouquet in the darker onion-skin-speckled wool. The darkest onion-skin oatmeal (usually the last layer of wool on the bottom of the pan) I used to fill in the basket. If you run short of the darker color, substitute a medium shade of tan for the basket sections.

White wool tinted with a light bath of walnut dye is also an acceptable antique color for the background. Use a slightly stronger walnut dye for the basket area and outlines. For complete dyeing directions with black walnuts, see "Making Brown Dye from Walnuts" in section III.

Dyeing the Border

The green outer band. The inner row of light green echoes the shades used in the leaves, as does the dark outer border. For 6 ounces of gray tweed or plaid (outer border), I used the following dye formula. Save ½ cup of this dye solution to dye the paler shade of green for the 4 ounces of the inner band.

For the border's gray herringbone, tweed, checks, or plaid (6 ounces), use the following:

^{3}/32 teaspoon of Dark Green
^{3}/32 teaspoon of Reseda Green
^{1}/32 teaspoon of Bright Green
^{3}/32 teaspoon of Bronze Green
1 tablespoon of salt

Simmer all these dyes and the salt in a 2-gallon dye pot. Remove ½ cup of the dye solution for the inner band. You want the gray textured material to be completely and evenly dyed. Add the presoaked wools and simmer fifteen minutes. Add ¼ cup of white vinegar and simmer for fifteen more minutes. Wash, rinse, and dry the wool.

The green inner-border band. You have reserved ½ cup of simmering dye for the inner-border band of green. Presoak 4 ounces of white wool. Add the dye to a 1-gallon dye pot filled half full of water. Crowd the presoaked wool in the simmering dye bath and continue to simmer for half an hour. Permit the wool to cool in the dye bath. Wash, rinse, and dry the wool.

The medium rosy-red line. Presoak 2 ounces of white wool. Use ^{1}/32 teaspoon of Terra Cotta dye and ½ teaspoon of salt for your dye solution. This is the same dye formula as the medium rose color dyed for the rose bowls. Crowd the wool into a 1-quart pan to mottle it. Simmer this for thirty minutes, permitting it to cool in the dye bath for complete take-up. Wash, rinse, and dry the wool.

Final Preparations

Your dyeing is now complete. You should have many shades of pinks, rosy-reds, and olive greens. Be sure to throw them down on the floor on top of your background oatmeal color before cutting them. Any color that gets lost against the background can be corrected now, rather than ripped out later. Roll your rose shades together to see if they all blend and are of differing values. Also, fold the shades of leaf greens together to check for graduations of color.

Before beginning to hook your rug, see the directions on cutting the wool in section II. Cut one half of each color of wool used in "Antique Flower Basket," and place the strips in clear plastic bags. Label the bags with a permanent marker to avoid confusion. I label my bags with the name of the section (i.e., leaf, rose, tulip); then I number each bag with the color value from light to dark required for each leaf or flower. For example, leaf green would be labeled #1-#7.

I always make a numbered color chart listing the area to be hooked, dye formula used, and amount required, including a swatch of that particular color for future reference. Using this system, I can identify the part, hook it with the correct color, and do the other similar flowers and leaves at the same time in different parts of the rug.

For this rug I bag each flower as a whole unit. Small plastic sandwich bags, filled and labeled with a number from my color chart, are stuffed into a larger plastic bag labeled with the name of the flower and the flower number. I make many rugs of one design in a year, but you may take a year to complete one rug. In both cases, labeling helps us remember.

Keep all the small leftover cutoff strips for flower highlights. This rug uses many little pieces. I keep a candy box for small strips (under 6 inches) beside my hooking table and drop in the snips as I go.

Hooking "Antique Flower Basket"

The rug will be hooked all over the place to avoid handling the same bags of color again and again. You should be an experienced rug hooker to tackle this design and should therefore have no trouble with maintaining tension on the foundation.

Hooking the Basket

Begin with the basket. One row of black wool will create the wires and base. Outline the entire basket, starting with the base. Hook from the base up the wires and around each top curve and then cut your strip, rather than attempting all those top semicircular curves at once. Repeat each wire from the base to the top, curving your top row. After completing the upright wires, hook the sideways wires. Here again, I skip over the single row of black loops (give a good tug to flatten out the underside bump) and continue from one side to the other side of the basket to eliminate tiny cut pieces.

Having finished the wire basket, fill in with the darker oatmeal-colored wool. You will find that one of the dark leaves droops over the top of the center of the basket. Hook in the leaf outline with the #5 medium dark leaf green before returning to the basket. Also outline the blue flower petals that touch the top of the basket.

Hooking the Blue Flowers

Hook in the gold flower centers. Outline each petal with the dark blue wool, beginning in the center. Avoid a double row of dark blue where petals touch. Complete hooking the blue flowers with the medium blue wool.

Hooking the Carnations

Outline the carnations with the rosy-red Terra Cotta–dyed wool from the border line. You have three close values of pink and six sections of the carnation. Alternate light, medium, and dark twice to fill these six sections. I know that the petals would logically shade from dark (bottom of the carnation) to light (top of the carnation), but nobody ever said primitive rugs were logical.

Hooking the Roses

I like to make each rose slightly different, as did early rug-makers. Begin with the lighter rose at the top of the rug. Hook the spiral in dark Terra-Cotta (posy) wool. Begin at the center and hook out. Leave a ¼-inch space between the spirals for one row of hooking. Fill in that space with a short piece of carnation pink from your refuse box. Outline the rose bowl and outer frill with Old Gold wool. Hook in the bowl with medium rose #2. Hook in the spots in the frill with dark rose #3, posy wool, Old Gold wool, or a combination of all three.

To hook the bottom rose, again begin with the dark Terra-Cotta spiral. Fill in the spiral with dark rose #3. Hook the frill with Old Gold, and fill in with medium rose #2. Hook the dark Terra-Cotta line (using posy wool) that defines the bowl. Hook the spots with all the snips you have in the snippet box: Old Gold, light rose, and carnation pink. Fill in the bowl with dark rose #3. The outer row of petals will be hooked in light rose #1. You need this light contrast against the oatmeal background.

Hooking the Posies

Hook in the center blue pod in two shades of flower blue (see your scrap box). Outline the pink petals in medium rose #2. Fill in those petals with carnation pink leftovers. Hook the remaining alternate petals with dark Terra Cotta. Alternate the stamens in Nugget Gold wool and dark Terra-Cotta wool. You need strong contrasts so that these small areas will show up against the background. Use your lightest and brightest Nugget Gold strips. Old Gold strips disappear.

Hooking the Tulips

The tulips use scraps from the other flowers. Begin with the center petal. Use the plaid stem material and outline the petal starting at the sepal. Hook around the petal and continue to finish the stem. Next, make one row of light leaf green #2 and fill in that center petal with lightest leaf green #1.

Side petals require three shades of rose. Begin with one row of dark Terra Cotta (posy wool), then hook two rows of dark rose #3, and finish the outside area with one row of medium rose #2. The inner petals are also hooked with medium rose #2.

Hooking the Grapes

Hook the center stem with brown plaid before hooking the grapes. Alternate shades of lavender and mauve. I hope you have overdyed to achieve several shades. Outline and hook in each grape before making the tiny stems. Hook from the grape to the central stem. If one grape stem is directly opposite another one, cross over the central stem and hook from grape to grape. This is a hooking sin, but rather one tiny bump (pull tightly with a tug) than two tiny strips.

Hooking the Leaf Stems and Veins

You have already hooked in some of the stems. Now complete all the stems and veins before beginning the leaves.

I hope you have scraps of various dark green and dark brown plaid or tweed wool. Tweeds and herringbones make great stems and veins. Before rug hookers knew any better, they cut up antique paisley shawls for these small areas! I have been given several old remnants by an eighty-year-old rug hooker. The colors are fine, but the overshot weave and the light weight of the fabric make this source of veins unacceptable for more reasons than one.

As I mentioned earlier, hideous colors can be overdyed to make acceptable stems and veins. Because you are using one color against both light and dark green, choose a middle tone. I used rust herringbone overdyed with Golden Brown.

Hooking the Leaves

The giant leaves alternate light and dark green. Some are hooked half-and-half, others, medium to darkest green, still others, light to medium green. Make a drawing of these three varieties, noting their color divisions, ahead of time so their hooking is not confusing to you.

For the darkest leaves, outline one row in #7 darkest green. Next, use two rows of #6 color. Then fill in the center around the veins in #5 medium dark.

For the medium leaves, outline one row of #4 dark medium green. Then hook one row of #3 medium green and two rows of #2 light green, filling in around the veins in #1 lightest green.

For the half-and-half leaves, start on the dark side. Outline one row of #7 darkest green. Then hook two rows of #6 dark green, and finish filling in around the veins with #5 medium dark green. On the light side, outline two rows of #1 lightest green. Then hook one row of #2 light green and one row of #3 medium green, and fill in around the veins in #4 dark medium green.

To fill in the small leaves, I use medium shades of green (#3 and #4). Outline with one row of #5 before hooking the leaf.

In hooking the leaves, be sure that the same colors do not run into each other. Some of the large leaves do overlap. Plan your leaves so that the same colors do not touch.

Hooking the Background

Begin hooking the background by outlining the entire composition in darker (or onion-skin-speckled) oatmeal wool. You may need to use the lighter shade of oatmeal background around the grapes if they disappear. Your eye will tell you if the contrast is not great enough.

Before beginning the background, hook in the pale green border, which will keep your rug straight. Sharpen the corners by hooking one extra loop before turning direction. Two sideways loops equal one forward loop.

Outline inside the border edge with several rows of oatmeal before beginning to hook around the outlined flower arrangement. You will get in tight little corners, but follow the forms and work your way out to the outside edge. Throw in some dark outline pieces now and then to enliven the background. The mellow warm hues of onion-speckled oatmeal will soften and highlight the background, keeping it from being a solid mass.

Remember to hook in your initials and the date before completing the background.

Finishing the Border

Hook in a single line of rosy-red from whatever store of medium reds you have left. Hook four or five rows of #7 darkest green (preferably dyed over gray tweed or herringbone wool for a very rich, dark, textured green). To finish hemming your rug, see the instructions in section VIII.

PATTERN ───────────────────────────────

"American Fruit Piece"

34 by 25 inches

Watermelon

Fruit. Two shades of Egyptian Red, light and medium.
Rind. Lightest value of Reseda Green.
Shell. Two shades of Dark Green with spot-dyed (Nugget Gold) stripes.

Pears

Light Old Gold plus a pinch of Nugget Gold. Spot-dye small scraps with light Egyptian Red for the blush.

Apples

Yellow apple. Medium shade of Old Gold plus a pinch of Nugget Gold; overdye small scraps with light Reseda Green for shading.
Green apple. Reseda Green plus a spot of apple yellow.
Red apple. Three shades of Egyptian Red: dark, medium, and light.

Peaches

Dark Brown pits overdyed on checked material. Use light Orange plus Egyptian Red in two shades; overdye a small scrap with Nugget Gold for highlights. Use camel for the crease and shadow.

Grapes

Very light Copenhagen Blue for the outlines. Add a grain of Egyptian Red to some of the above scraps to make top center outlines. Use lightest blue for highlights on grapes. Grape centers are all shades of navy from bright (center) to dark at the bottom and sides of grape cluster.

Cherries

Dark Egyptian Red, with light red highlights.

Strawberries

Medium Egyptian Red, with Nugget Gold seeds.

Cantaloupe

Very light Old Gold overdyed and spotted with pale Reseda Green. Add slightly more green dye for small shadows under the pears. Dividing lines are "peach" orange.

Leaves

Many shades of Reseda Green for the various leaves, overdyeing on neutral checks and plaids.

Use Olive Green plus Reseda Green or Dark Green (or both) for the four shades of grape leaves and veins. Add a pinch of Nugget Gold to brighten one or all of the shades. Alternate dark veins on light leaf centers and light veins on dark leaf centers for change and contrast.

Medium Dark Green was used for strawberry leaves. Overdye a plaid or check to variegate the tiny areas. Using Dark Green scraps from the watermelon shell for leaf veins will carry this shade of green throughout the composition.

Stems and Tendrils

Spot-dye camel scraps with onion skins to give variety to the single rows.

Background

Shades of black, solid and antique, were mixed for the background of the rug. Overdyeing scraps of bright colors with Black dye will add a faint glimmer of color.

Border

One row of Nugget Gold, four rows of the melon green, and five rows of Reseda Green overdyed on neutral checks.

D Y E S
(W. Cushing & Co.)

Egyptian Red

Reseda Green

Dark Green

Olive Green

Black

Dark Brown (optional)

Nugget Gold

Old Gold

Orange

Copenhagen Blue

Navy Blue

"American Fruit Piece" is an adaptation of an 1859 Currier &
Ives print. The luscious watermelon in the center of the design
is surrounded by grapes, peaches, cherries, apples, pears,
strawberries, and a large cantaloupe. This design is reminis-
cent of early theorem paintings stencilled on velvet.

"American Fruit Piece" is not a beginner rug, so I have not
attempted to give complete dyeing or hooking directions. An
expert rugmaker can choose her colors and dye from experi-
ence. I will give general dyeing instructions and hooking procedures. See section II for complete dyeing instructions.

You may decide to enlarge this rug pattern to any size from
the original 34 by 25 inches; remember that four times the
area will provide sufficient material.

This rug requires a #8 cut (¼-inch-wide strips), but a #6 cut
was used where noted. Finer cuts can render the objects with a
greater degree of shading than I have described here.

Planning the Color Scheme

Because "American Fruit Piece" employs so many colors, it is
wise to use the same dyes in many combinations to give an
overall compatible tone to the finished rug.

When planning your color distribution, remember to contrast light against dark so that the sections will not get lost.
Working with a black background gives the warm colors a
sense of richness. Medium and light tones show up best against
the dark background.

Three or four shades of a color are enough for this primitive rug. Use various checks and plaids in greens or neutrals
when dyeing leaves to give small areas a variegated look. This
will eliminate the need for shading. Dye these textured wools
along with the small quantities needed to complete the leaves
of each fruit.

Mottled or spot dyeing is also valuable in enlivening small
leaves. Vary the Reseda Green by adding pinches of Dark
Green, Nugget Gold, or Olive Green to each small dye bath so
that the leaves of each fruit are related.

The grape leaves can be dyed with the same technique, or
use three or four graduated shades of Olive Green (plus small
specks of Reseda Green, Dark Green, or Nugget Gold).

In this way, too, add a pinch of Nugget Gold to the Dark

Green watermelon shell to give more life to the color, or spot dye the Dark Green with Nugget Gold in the original dyebath.

General Dyeing Directions

Dye small quantities of each color listed. Because the amounts needed are so tiny, plan to dye in sequence for three or four shades of each color. You can dip dye or dye in sequential order, darkest to lightest.

Use salt for a mordant, as vinegar will make a fast takeup and brighten the colors too much.

Refer to section II for more details on dyeing techniques and procedures.

Hooking "American Fruit Piece"

It is easier to plan your hooking progress by first hooking the objects that are in the foreground of the design. Because of overlapping, you will have to skip around the rug rather than begin immediately in the center. This means the grape cluster and leaf drooping over the watermelon will have to be hooked first. The pear stem and leaves are next.

Hooking the Grapes

Outline all grapes with #6 cut. Use the deepest shade of Copenhagen Blue for the lower grape outline and graduate to a lighter shade of blue to outline the top center grapes. This change in value will contour the grape cluster automatically. Light areas come forward, dark areas recede. Use many shades of navy for the grapes and insert a #6 cut spot of pale blue to highlight each grape.

Hooking the Watermelon

Hook the watermelon seeds in black with one white seed somewhere in the center. Beginning with the lightest shade of Reseda Green, hook one row of rind, one row of the next darker shade of Reseda Green, one row of medium green, and one row of Dark Green. This will complete the rind.

Begin hooking the inside of the watermelon with lightest Egyptian Red. Then intermingle the light medium shades, progressing to the darkest shade of watermelon pink as it touches the shell, so that the heart of the fruit is the deepest shade.

Outline the shell with Dark Green and make rows of Dark Green and Dark Green plus Nugget Gold for the watermelon stripes.

I find it easier to complete the yellow apple and pears before completing the lower half of the watermelon shell. This helps you maintain the shape of these fruits before you complete the rest of the watermelon shell.

You may hook in the various leaves as you go, or leave them all until the end before completing the background. If you plan to wait to hook the leaves—sometimes this approach is better for color planning—be sure to outline each leaf as you go to protect its shape.

Hooking the Pears
Outline the pears in the deepest shade of Old Gold–Nugget Gold, reserving the overlapping area for a camel shadow. Choose the area of blush and hook in a highlight, then fill in each pear following the contour of the fruit.

Hooking the Yellow Apple
Begin with the camel stems and black cup. Choose the highlight area and hook in the palest shade of Nugget Gold and melon green. Outline the apple with the deepest shade of apple yellow and, following the contour, complete the fruit, graduating to medium apple yellow.

Hooking the Peaches
Use a dark brown tweed for the peach pits. Hook in the deepest shade of peach for one row of skin and medium peach for the cut fruit.

The peach overlapped by grapes must be shadowed with camel along that edge and in the crease. Use the brightest shade of peach (plus gold) for the blush and fill in with medium peach.

Hooking the Cherries
Continue around the composition by hooking the cherries darkest Egyptian Red and highlight with #6 cut of palest red. The tiny stems are palest green or camel (#6 cut).

Hooking the Green and Red Apples

As with the yellow apple, hook in the stem and cup. Outline the green apple with medium Reseda Green, using the deepest shade for the shadow between the peach and yellow apple. Add a highlight of apple yellow and fill in with medium green.

Repeat the same procedure for the red apple using the deepest Egyptian Red behind the other apples and graduating to medium Egyptian Red in the center. Add a light red highlight.

Hooking the Strawberries

Hook several seeds in each strawberry with Nugget Gold (#6 cut). Fill in the berries with medium Egyptian Red.

Hooking the Cantaloupe

Hook deep peach lines to contour the cantaloupe. Using the deepest apple green, hook the area shadowed by the pears. Then, following the contours of the melon, hook vertically, outlining each section first, ending in the center.

If you have not done so already, finish hooking the watermelon shell. Save the deepest Dark Green shade for the areas around the fruits and leaves.

Hooking the Stems and Tendrils

Hook the tendrils and remaining grape stem with onion-spotted camel. Use a #8 cut so that single lines will not get lost.

Hooking the Leaves

Each variety of fruit should have a different green cast to its leaves. Use watermelon green for the various veins. For variety, use some light veins in the grape leaves, contrasted with darker green in the center, graduating to medium green in the outline. Curled leaves will be lighter on the back side to contrast with the front of the leaf.

Hooking the Background

Having completed the center of the rug, outline each leaf and fruit with solid black. This will provide the greatest contrast against the colored wools. Outline the rectangular background edges with several rows of black before beginning to hook in the background area with antique and solid black wool. Place your initials and the date in the bottom corners with a shade of medium green.

Finishing the Border

Hook one gold row, four rows of melon green, and five rows of medium Reseda Green.

To finish the rug, overcast the folded edges with black or green yarn and add cotton rug tape. To hem your rug, see the instructions in section VIII.

Hemming Your Rug

VIII

Your rug is finished and is now ready to be hemmed. The burlap edges must be carefully handled so that they do not unravel during the binding process.

Binding Yarn

I always use a binding of wool yarn, either a crewel wool or a knitting worsted yarn (four-ply). Crewel wool is beautiful and comes in many colors, but you may dye it to match the border when dyeing your border material. This weight yarn takes up ten times the perimeter of your rug. Several ounces will bind a two-by-three-foot rug.

If you do not choose to dye or spend the money for crewel yarn, knitting worsted (four-ply) is an excellent choice of yarn for binding. I was lucky enough to buy pounds of wool carpet yarn from a junkyard dealer years ago when carpets were still woven with wool. Knitting worsted works every bit as well and has the added strength of synthetic yarns. Be careful that the yarn does not shine; some synthetics do. I use 75 percent olefin and 25 percent acrylic yarn, which is perfect and inexpensive.

Cotton Rug Tape

Use cotton rug tape to finish binding your rug. It comes in many colors and may be ordered by the yard. When I dye the border's wool, I like to dye my tape to match. Cotton does not take the dye as readily as wool, so it may dye lighter. Jack up your dye bath a bit for the cotton rug tape.

Plan to buy a little more rug tape than the perimeter of your finished rug, as binding does shrink when washed and you need several inches more for mitering the corners and overlaps. Be aware that deep colors in rug tape run, which is another reason to wash your tape before binding. Never, ever, use iron-on rug tape.

Having gathered your wool and rug tape, you will need to have the following:

crewel or yarn needle

large-eyed sharp needle

sharp scissors

straight pins with china heads or T pins

buttonhole thread or dual-purpose thread to match your wool and tape

Pressing Your Rug

First press the finished rug with a damp cloth and hot iron. The wet cloth (not a commercial ironing cloth) will create steam when ironed on top of the rug face. I use a piece of old sheet. Never use a steam iron directly on the wool face. You need to use slight pressure and lots of steam, so keep wetting the pressing cloth, wringing out the excess water, and steam pressing the whole top face of the rug. The ironing will smooth out uneven loops (if there are any) and flatten the rug for smooth binding. Permit the rug to dry flat on the floor before proceeding.

Cutting the Excess Foundation

Lay the rug facedown on a counter or table so that it is completely flat. Fold over the remaining burlap edge until it is ¼ inch from the edge of the last row of hooked loops. Pin the burlap in place with china-headed pins or T pins. Dressmaker pins sometimes get lost in the hem. The ¼-inch folded edge will be bound with yarn.

You may cut off the excess burlap 1¼ inch from the folded edge now or wait until the rug is bound with yarn. It is easier to miter the rug corners when the excess foundation is removed, but if you are worried about the cut burlap edge unraveling, wait to trim until later.

Binding the Rug with Yarn

Thread the yarn needle with a length of yarn comfortable for you to pull through the burlap. I cut mine about 18 inches long.

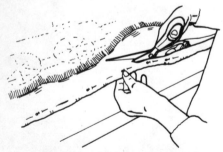

Cut off the excess burlap 1¼ inches from the edge of the rug. Do NOT cut away the burlap to the edge. Your cotton rug tape is 1¼ inches wide. You will hide the raw burlap directly under the cotton rug tape and sew it down along with the tape to the rug.

Using a running stitch, begin by working the yarn through the burlap hem before beginning to overcast the edge. I leave a 3-inch *unknotted* end to tie in later. Work from the back of the rug.

Begin to overcast the ¼-inch burlap fold at the outer edge of your rug. Work one overcast stitch directly against the other so no burlap is visible. Continue overcasting until you run out of yarn. End by running the yarn into the burlap hem. Rethread your needle and make several running stitches to the loose end. Knot this yarn to the new length in a square knot that will be hidden in the hem before running your needle back up to the edge and continuing to overcast. Use the same knotting procedure for each new length of yarn, and finish by knotting in the first end with the last thread. Keep the knots away from the overcast edge so they will be hidden by the rug tape.

Old-time rugmakers sometimes folded the burlap edge back before they finished hooking the border and then hooked through two thicknesses of burlap to hem the rug. Disaster! I have tried to repair this sure-to-wear-out-first edge and have had to unravel several inches into the rug itself to rehem the edge. This is why you so often see a strip of fabric binding antique rug edges—a repair job.

Sewing the Rug Tape

Having completed the yarn binding, you are now ready to add the cotton rug tape. If you have not already done so, cut off the excess burlap 1¼ inch from the edge that is pinned into place. Begin to stitch the cotton rug tape to the newly bound yarn edge with buttonhole-twist or heavy-duty thread (to match). Use a blind stitch. Keep the stitches close to each other and to the yarn-bound edge so no burlap is visible.

Begin at a corner and stitch around the entire rug, mitering each corner. You will have folded the burlap in each corner so it will not be unduly bulky under the tape. Under no circumstances should you trim all this corner burlap away. Corners take hard wear and burlap unravels easily, as do linen and cotton rug foundations.

End at the last corner, overlapping the cotton tape and folding back the hem. Now sew down the inside edge of the rug tape to the back of the rug. You will catch the scant edge of

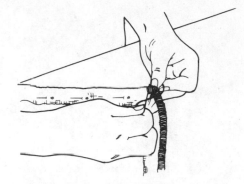

When rounding the corner with the yarn, fold over the burlap into a miter, but do not trim to the edge. Make several extra stitches at each corner to be sure the burlap is covered.

As you stitch around the inside edge of the tape, sew in your mitered corners. End with an overlapping hem and sew it securely to the edge of the binding.

the burlap hem as you stitch the tape to the back of the loops. Be sure not to pull these loops or dig too deeply with your needle, or the stitch will show on the face of the rug.

To complete your beautiful hooked rug, sew a nametag (if you have one) onto the cotton rug tape for identification in future years. You have created a family heirloom!

The Care of Hand-Hooked Rugs

IX

All hand-hooked rugs, regardless of their foundations, must be handled with care. The basic chain stitch, which is what hooking is, can pull out easily with the sharp claws of pets. These animals must not nest in your rugs. Most of the rugs I repair were attacked by animal claws. Hooked rugs, on the other hand, are easy to repair. Save the strips and rehook into the torn-out area. If you need additional strips, try to match them—one good reason to save some of every color that you have used. If you cannot match them, primitive hooked rugs can be repaired with make-dos. Old rugs frequently display areas of mismatched color, anyway.

Another scourge of hooked rugs is the vagrant thread; if pulled, it rips out an entire area. Clip threads, do not pull them. Odd ends popping out of the bottom should be pulled to the top side and clipped off. A hooking crossover on the bottom side is a prime reason for ripping. If crossovers do occur in the making of a rug, and I have advocated a few in this book's patterns, pull extra hard with a good tug when hooking the spot to ensure a flat bottom that is not likely to snag.

Cleaning Your Hooked Rug

Vacuum cleaners (oh, horrors, not an upright!) can chew up a rug at once. Use a hand vacuum or a canister vacuum cleaner with a small nozzle brush set on the least amount of suction for your biweekly cleaning. I open all the vents on my sweeper for very weak suction. Hooked rugs on the floor in an area of low traffic do not need strenuous cleaning methods. Do not shake or beat a hooked rug, regardless of what your grandmother has told you. The violent action can snap burlap foundation threads. Antique rugs hooked on burlap bags or left uncared for in hot attics or moldy basements are particularly susceptible to damage from violent cleaning practices. Don't let an old-timer tell you to place a hooked rug in the snow and sweep it clean. This old wives' tale has been debunked by modern cleaning methods.

Wall-hung rugs, protected from leaping cats—I repaired one of these accidents—are not dust or dirt catchers and can be vacuumed infrequently.

Storing a Hooked Rug

Never fold a rug; always roll it. Store an unused hooked rug top side out when rolling it up. Rolling the rug with the loops inside puts a terrible strain on the burlap foundation. Store rugs in a comfortable environment, such as your living quarters, neither too hot and dry nor too cold and damp. Burlap becomes brittle with age if not treated as kindly as you would treat yourself.

Avoid plastic bags for storing rugs. Wrap the rug loosely loop side out in an old sheet or in acid-free tissue paper (available at any art store). Do not secure with rubber bands or any tight fastening. Rugs need to breathe, just as people do.

Special Cleaning Tips

We have discussed everyday cleaning and caring for your rug, but what about a really dirty rug that needs drastic measures? First and foremost—do NOT send your hooked rug to a commercial dry cleaner to be cleaned. Commercial rug-cleaning establishments have no idea what a hooked rug is. If they consider it an Oriental, they will wash it and ruin the hand if not pull it apart altogether. I have had a rug returned for resuscitation after it suffered at the hands of the best rug-cleaning establishment in New York. The cleaner had washed it, ruining the foundation, and it had lost all its bounce. The poor limp thing was beyond hope.

The wool can, however, be surface cleaned. As most wool was previously washed prior to hooking, it will not bleed. I have spot cleaned dirty, sticky spots from pets and food with a mild detergent. Whip up the foam and, using a sponge, gently moisten the spot to dissolve the hard residues. Then sponge the spot again, rubbing very gently to dislodge the dirt. Use a cloth or sponge dipped in clear water to remove the foam and then blot the rug dry.

Full cleaning jobs can be done with this same surface method for light soil. There is now a commercial hooked-rug cleaner on the market for more serious soil, available at rug supply houses.

Repairing an Old Hooked Rug

Old rugs, with years of questionable care, will become dry and brittle. When these foundation fibers break, rehooking in the area is impossible, as the base continues to crack with the added strain. I have tried adding a patch of new burlap and rehooking into it, but the adjoining burlap was weak as well and continued to break.

It is better to line the rug or the small area with a loosely woven kettle cloth or prewashed muslin, then sew the loops back into the new foundation with small stitches onto the base. This section will appear as a hooked area on the face of the rug if care is taken to keep the pile a consistent height with the rest of the loops.

Full linings of hooked rugs catch soil and grind against the loops inside if the rugs are underfoot. These linings are better suited to repairing and preserving wall hangings.

Hanging Your Rug

You can hang a rug temporarily by using café curtain rings sewed to the top edge of the binding. In time, however, the rug will sag from its own weight, putting strain on the ring areas. Support the full weight of the hooked rug on a dowel stick or metal rod, available from drapery suppliers. It will evenly distribute the weight and avoid undue strain on any section of the rug.

Sew a cuff of fabric or another strip of cotton rug tape to the top finished edge of the rug. This sleeve will provide a slot for your dowel rod. Attach the rod with drapery fasteners to the wall, or use bent nails or cup hooks.

An expensive and more permanent method of hanging a large rug is to sew Velcro on three sides, leaving the bottom open. Tack or glue the opposite Velcro side to a frame made to fit the size of the rug. By applying gentle pressure, the rug can be pressed onto the frame. Do not stretch the rug too tightly, or you may damage the foundation fibers. For this reason, I do not recommend stretching a lined hooked rug to a frame as you would stretch a canvas. Rugs need to have give to accommodate the slight shrinking and stretching that occurs with changes in humidity and temperature. They are living works of art made from natural materials and swell and relax like paper or any natural fabric. For the same reason, do not staple, nail, or glue a rug to a frame or board, and never place it behind glass or plastic.

Backings for Your Rug

Finally, if you are using your rug on the floor, always use a rug pad. I like a ¼-inch foam pad cut slightly smaller than the rug to hide the offending edge. Thicker rug pads will raise the rug off the floor and expose the pad but are valuable in high-traffic areas.

An odious latex backing is sold to paint on the back of hooked rugs. Theoretically, it is supposed to prevent loops from pulling out. Never use latex backing! It is recommended for yarn punched rugs, but I have been asked to repair old rugs backed with this stuff, and it has turned to cement. Time will harden and crack it, destroying any rug that has been so painted.

Treat your rug with loving care. It was made in this spirit and will last for generations if properly cared for.

Sources of Supplies

Instructional videos:
Pat Hornafius
113 Meadowbrook Lane
Elizabethtown, PA 17022
(717) 367-7706

"How to Hook a Traditional Hand Hooked Rug"
A complete description of rug making that includes planning
the rug, hooking techniques, and hemming the finished rug.
Equipment needed and sources are included.
60 minutes VHS
$30 U.S. plus $3 UPS or $3.50 U.S. and Canada (parcel post)

"Dyeing for Rugs: Natural and Commercial Dyes"
A description of dyeing techniques and equipment needed for
natural dyes (walnut, goldenrod, marigolds, and onion skins)
and commercial dyes (Cushing dyes).
40 minutes VHS
$30 U.S. plus $3 UPS or $3.50 U.S. and Canada (parcel post)

Patterns described in this book:
Pat Hornafius
113 Meadowbrook Lane
Elizabethtown, PA 17022
(717) 367-7706
All are silk-screened on 10-ounce even-weave primitive burlap
suitable for #8 or #6 cut.
$25 U.S. per pattern plus $3 UPS or $3.50 U.S. and Canada
(parcel post)

The sources listed here provide supplies for primitive rug making. Please specify "primitive" when ordering.

Most companies have catalogs, but please send along a self-addressed stamped business-sized envelope for answers to inquiries.

Braid-Aid
466 Washington Street
Pembroke, MA 02359
(617) 826-2560
Complete hooking supplies.

Dorr Mill Store
P.O. Box 88
Guild, NH 03754-0088
(603) 863-1197
Complete hooking supplies.

Forestheart Studio
21 South Carroll Street
Frederick, MD 21701
(301) 695-4815 or 663-3855
Linen rug backing.

Harry M. Fraser Co.
R&R Machine Co.
Route 3, Box 254-1A
Stoneville, NC 27048
(919) 573-9830
Bliss Strip Slitter and complete hooking supplies.

Heirloom Care
P.O. Box 2540
Westwood, MA 02090
(617) 762-2177
Heirloom Care hooked-rug cleaner.

Joan Moshimer's Rug Hooker Studio
P.O. Box 351
North Street
Kennebunkport, ME 04046
Complete hooking supplies and Cushing dyes.

Mandy's Wool Shed
Rt. 1, Box 2680
Litchfield, ME 04350
(207) 582-5059
Wool.

Mayflower Textiles
P.O. Box 329
Franklin, MA 02038
Puritan rug frames.

J. D. Paulsen
P.O. Box 158
Bridgton, ME 14009
Rigby cutters.

Mrs. Chalmer C. Van Horn
R.D. #4
Box 340
Munsy, PA 17756
Woolrich wool.

Index